Teach®
Yourself

CVs
In A Week

David McWhir

First published in Great Britain in 2012 by Hodder Education. An Hachette UK company.

This edition published in 2016 by John Murray Learning

Copyright © David McWhir 2012, 2016

The right of David McWhir to be identified as the Author of the Work has been asserted by him in accordance with the Copyright, Designs and Patents Act 1988.

Database right Hodder & Stoughton (makers)

The *Teach Yourself* name is a registered trademark of Hachette UK.

British Library Cataloguing in Publication Data: a catalogue record for this title is available from the British Library.

ISBN: 978 147 3 60943 3
eISBN: 978 144 4 15930 1

1

The publisher has used its best endeavours to ensure that any website addresses referred to in this book are correct and active at the time of going to press. However, the publisher and the author have no responsibility for the websites and can make no guarantee that a site will remain live or that the content will remain relevant, decent or appropriate.

The publisher has made every effort to mark as such all words which it believes to be trademarks. The publisher should also like to make it clear that the presence of a word in the book, whether marked or unmarked, in no way affects its legal status as a trademark.

Every reasonable effort has been made by the publisher to trace the copyright holders of material in this book. Any errors or omissions should be notified in writing to the publisher, who will endeavour to rectify the situation for any reprints and future editions.

Typeset by Cenveo Publisher Services.

Printed in Great Britain by CPI Group (UK) Ltd, Croydon, CR0 4YY.

John Murray Learning policy is to use papers that are natural, renewable and recyclable products and made from wood grown in sustainable forests. The logging and manufacturing processes are expected to conform to the environmental regulations of the country of origin.

John Murray Learning
Carmelite House
50 Victoria Embankment
London EC4Y 0DZ
www.hodder.co.uk

Also available in ebook

Contents

Introduction

Alongside your passport, your CV is one of the most important documents you possess. In many ways, it is as important as your passport, enabling someone at a gateway to decide whether you can pass to the next stage of your career. Unlike a passport, however, a CV is a document that you can strengthen and develop as your career progresses. In fact, the phrase *curriculum vitae,* for which CV is an abbreviation, means 'life path'. Look after your CV and its accurate representation of your career achievements will serve you well as you move to new career challenges.

This book will help you build, maintain and navigate your way around your own successful CV. Career-wise it remains the single most important means of getting yourself noticed and in you reaching that critical first-stage interview.

As well as having a behavioural sciences degree and having consulted to a large number of public, private and not-for-profit organizations across the world, I have spent many years in business as a manager, sifting through CVs, and will share with you the key elements of a CV that make it stand out (for the right reasons).

Prospective employers vary widely in the degree of sophistication they apply in assessing CVs as the first stage of finding the right job candidate. Increasingly, organizations are turning to professional recruitment agencies to undertake the first stage of assessment. A number of others have started to use software to pick up on key words and phrases in electronically submitted CVs. What is clear is that, in economically challenging times, organizations are necessarily ruthless in reducing the high volumes of CVs they receive down to manageable numbers. In order to stand a realistic chance of passing through this rigorous first stage, your CV must be extremely well constructed, concise and relevant.

Refer to this book every time you amend your CV (which, as we shall see, should be done every time you apply for a new role), and this discipline will ensure that you give yourself the best means of portraying your skills, experience and most important qualities in a way that managers and the increasingly used external recruitment agencies expect.

A proportion of what is contained in this book may fall under what can be called common sense. In my time, however, I have seen many CVs that do not even come close to meeting what would be called minimum standards. I have therefore included every relevant detail I can think of, whether obvious to me or not, in the hope that it will help you get the role you desire.

I will use the term 'CV' throughout this book as a description of the document initially presented to a potential employer, in which you describe your career and achievements to date. In some cultures and countries, such a document is referred to as a resumé (or résumé) and there is some debate as to differences between the two documents. However, any differences are essentially a matter of style rather than in core content.

Throughout the course of this book, I will also refer to the role applied for as a 'position', 'job' or 'vacancy' and in doing so I am referring to the same thing. I will also refer to the organization to which you apply for a role by a range of descriptions, simply for the sake of variety. Therefore, terms such as 'employer', 'prospective employer', 'employing organization' and 'potential employer' mean the same thing. However, it is worth pointing out at this stage that a CV or similar representation of one's skills, experience and achievements is equally important for the increasing number of people who operate as self-employed or agency personnel looking to win contracts or other types of work where any type of selection process is involved.

David McWhir

SUNDAY

Planning a successful CV

Today we will explore what organizations generally look for when assessing the CVs they receive for a particular role. Due to demographics and challenging economic pressures, securing a role, whether it is your first position or a step up in your career, is increasingly competitive. We therefore focus on how to increase the odds of your CV getting you through to the critical first interview stage.

The truth is that no matter how good your interview and interpersonal skills, one small error in your CV could prevent you having the opportunity to demonstrate those skills to a potential employer.

In this chapter we will look at:

- points to consider before you start to write your CV
- how a prospective employer will typically deal with your CV.

The press often carries stories about seemingly industrious and committed individuals who have submitted tens if not hundreds of CVs (or to be more accurate, the same CV tens or hundreds of times) but appear unlucky not to have secured even one interview from their efforts. Is this indeed simply bad luck or is there something significantly amiss in their approach?

One of the problems in mass mailing the same CV to multiple organizations is that to the potential employer that is exactly what it looks like. It says to them that you are looking for any role and will take the first opportunity that comes along. While it is perfectly understandable for someone to adopt this approach if they are desperate to generate income, it is unlikely, other than in the most fortunate of circumstances, to get you the role that you desire. If you do secure a job using this technique, it is unlikely to be one that you will stay with for long, since the chances of your skills and the job's requirements matching will be slim – leading you or the organization to look for a way out.

Points to consider before creating your CV

You may feel under pressure to get a job, or increase your income by moving role and be tempted to take the mass numbers approach described above. However, you are more likely to be successful if you take the following key steps.

Step 1

Be absolutely honest with yourself about what you want to do in your life and what types of role you enjoy. Think about which roles you are suited to through your skills, qualifications, experience and personality.

You may not necessarily secure your ideal role immediately but knowing what you are aiming for and being able to articulate your career goals will make you a more plausible candidate, not only from your CV but in the event that you are successful in getting to the interview stage.

Step 2

Seek feedback from family and friends as to what they see as being your strengths as well as areas that you may need to work on. Having, and admitting to, aspects of performance you need to improve is absolutely acceptable. In fact, many organizations are particularly interested in individuals who have recognized areas of development in themselves *and* have done something to address them.

Step 3

Invest time in understanding what a potential employer is looking for when they publicize a job vacancy. If your skills and experience are well below or, indeed, well above the required levels, it is unlikely that your CV will get you through to the interview stage. Although it is tempting to manipulate the description of your skills and experience to those requested, any gaps are likely to be identified by a competent interviewer, or when you actually start in the role.

An active decision not to continue an application based on a ruthless appraisal of the job description for the role in question will be to your advantage in the long term, because you will then be more likely to focus on roles that do fit your career goals.

Step 4

Thoroughly research the employment sectors you are interested in. Most sectors have a range of specialist publications which not only include vacancies in that particular sector but carry articles on issues and trends of relevance to it. An awareness of current issues within the sector of interest to you will place you in a good light with a potential interviewer as well as helping you understand what types of achievement will be of particular interest in a CV.

Spend time getting to know individuals already employed in that sector or role. Find out how they got into their role; what skills and experience their employers find particularly attractive in their employees; what roles are in demand and which organizations appear to be growing stronger (or doing less well, and which you may wish to avoid).

Step 5

It is important that you keep your skills and experience current while you research your next career step. Even if you are already in a role and looking to move internally to a different role, an employer will welcome evidence that you have continued to improve your skills. Recruiters often use phrases such as 'drifted', 'coasted' or 'reached a plateau' to describe an applicant who appears from their CV to lack direction or purpose. It is vitally important that you are seen as proactive in the progression and ownership of your own career.

There are a number of skills that are core to many positions. These can be categorized broadly into:

● interpersonal and communication skills
● IT and computer literacy skills
● time and project management skills
● managing a budget.

Demonstration of increased competence in any of these aspects, together with proficiency in any specialist skills required, are positive aspects to be included in your CV.

How a prospective employer typically deals with your CV

From experience, I believe that there are up to five common stages of CV review that will determine whether you and your CV get to the next stage of the selection process – this normally meaning the first-stage interview.

Not all potential employers will follow all five stages and others may amalgamate or reorder two or more of these. However, if you test your CV against what follows, you will increase your chances in getting through to the next stage of the selection process.

The glance over

This is a very quick scan across the first page for 'look and feel'. It may stagger you to learn that many organizations can reduce the CV pile by up to 90 per cent at this stage, without the reviewer having read a complete sentence in the document. Indeed, some organizations and recruiters are now using software at the first stage in order to identify key words and phrases of interest as well as negative aspects such as spelling mistakes.

Reasons for rejection at this stage include the following.

- **Spelling errors** – even just one. Many CV reviewers can spot a spelling error the second they raise the document to read; it immediately catches their attention. The view runs that this is a document you have had time to craft and check before submitting to an organization as an indicator of you at your best. With resources such as online spell checkers, the traditional dictionary and a family member or friend to check your document, there is no excuse for spelling errors. These are often interpreted by CV reviewers as being from someone who has hurried through the exercise, has poor attention to detail or is indiscriminately churning out CVs by the dozen. Whichever way, these are not impressions that are seen positively by most potential employers.
- **Fonts** that are too small, difficult to read or in different colours. These just take too much effort to read. As such, a CV may be rejected within a few seconds, regardless of the skills or experience of the CV's owner.
- **Opening personal statements** that are not backed up by evidence – and usually exaggerated, often baffling and frequently written in the third person. Such statements are normally ignored but can be cause for immediate rejection if they are particularly clichéd or outrageous in their claims: *'Joe Smith is a dynamic and indomitable individual who is a huge asset to any team. He is simultaneously a team player while striving to lead those around him in surpassing objectives.'*

The read through

Having passed the 'glance over' stage, your CV will then be subject to a more studied and structured examination. Your challenge for this stage is to make the reviewer read your complete CV without finding cause for rejection.

SUNDAY

MONDAY

TUESDAY

WEDNESDAY

THURSDAY

FRIDAY

SATURDAY

What the reviewer is looking for in particular now is:

● the relevance of your skills and experience to the role, particularly those deemed essential for the job
● evidence/indicators of your ability to perform at the level of the role or, indeed, slightly above it
● indicators of your approach to work and general attitude.

To increase your chances of successfully navigating the 'read through' stage and getting to the interview stage, you may wish to use my **CAREER** acronym:

● **Complete:** Your CV should be up to date and cover your career achievements to date. Unexplained gaps are likely to lead to immediate rejection, so any periods of non-work such as family time or unemployment should be covered – be truthful and give reasons for these particular periods. The majority of organizations understand that such absences from work occur and are accepting of them if reasons are provided. Please do not mistake 'complete' for 'lengthy'. If the prospective employer requires further detail, they will ask for it at the interview stage; your CV needs to be succinct and accurate.
● **Authentic:** The one sure-fire way to get your CV rejected is to include material that is exaggerated or even completely untrue (in other words, a lie). Such an approach is likely to be uncovered at the interview stage when it becomes clear

that you cannot back up a statement. Even if inaccuracies are not identified and you do secure the position, it is still possible to be dismissed months, if not years, later if your CV is found to be inaccurate. This will cause problems not only for the current job but for future progression, because your employer may point out this issue to future potential employers seeking references.

- **Relevant:** As the next section explains, most positions are now defined by a job description, providing details of roles and responsibilities. The reviewer will be looking for the relevance and 'fit' of your CV to the job description for the position in question. It is important, therefore, that you invest time in reading and understanding the job description before tailoring and submitting your CV for this particular job.

Think about the roles you have undertaken and what you have achieved. How can you word these achievements to demonstrate how you can apply your successful approach to the requirements of the new role? Organizations continue to rely heavily on the view that previous behaviours are a reliable indicator of your future performance. If you can demonstrate that you are already performing many elements of the role for which you are applying, you will increase your chances of getting to the interview stage.

- **Evidenced:** Be prepared to back up at the interview stage any statements you make within your CV. Test each statement you make with a possible question that an interviewer might ask to 'go deeper' into a particular statement or element of your career to date. Think about how you will answer such questions on the basis of what you included in your CV. Assemble additional material that can be used to support your CV at the interview stage. Unless specifically asked to do so, you should not include such additional material with your CV. Instead, prepare it alongside your CV for use at the next stage.

> **TIP** *View your CV as a series of signposts that highlight different aspects and achievements in your career to date.*

At the interview stage, the interviewer may ask for further evidence to support statements you make in your CV. For example, you may say in your CV: 'I was the top performing sales person at my present organization in the previous year, beating my personal annual target by 25 per cent.' Assuming this statement is relevant to the role in question, such a statement is likely to make a positive impression on the CV reviewer and add support to the decision to ask you to attend an interview. At the interview stage, be prepared to provide documentation that confirms your statement and to answer questions that search behind the statement for evidence of your personal contribution to such an outcome: 'How did you achieve this result?' or 'What planning did you do and what steps did you take?'

- **Emotionally intelligent:** An increasingly important quality considered by potential employers is your ability to interact effectively with people around you. Even if the intended role involves a significant proportion of time working on your own, most employers are looking for individuals who can communicate effectively with customers, colleagues and their manager. Therefore, your CV should include evidence of your ability to interact with other individuals and of self-awareness, a key element of emotional intelligence.

For more information on this topic, I would recommend Daniel Goleman's book *Emotional Intelligence: Why It Can Matter More Than IQ* (Bloomsbury Publishing, 1996). There are also many articles and discussions on the Internet on this important topic.

● **Referenced:** Any elements you include in your CV should be capable of being backed up at the interview stage or via further reference checks by the potential employer. Information contained in your CV should be consistent with information a potential employer may obtain from previous employers and from other sources such as social media.

To help you plan your CV, try checking it against the CAREER acronym. Your successful CV should be:
Complete
Authentic
Relevant
Evidenced
Emotionally intelligent
Referenced

Validating your CV against role requirements

This stage may be wholly or partly incorporated within the read through described above but is one to consider very carefully when creating your CV. The majority of roles today are normally defined by a 'job description' detailing the roles and responsibilities of the job holder: what is expected of the job holder, to whom they report, how their performance will be measured and so on. The key point here is that the organization already has a very good idea of the type of person they require. It is fundamental to your chances of success that your CV matches the requirements of the role as stated in the job description as closely as possible.

Example job description

Company: Cool Vectors Inc.
Job title: Sales and Marketing Executive
Reporting to: Sales and Marketing Vice Principal, Alphaville
Based at: Cool Vectors Inc., Ivory Towers, Alphaville

Job purpose:
To plan, co-ordinate and execute direct marketing and sales activities, so as to maintain and develop sales of CV Inc.'s Vector Tool range to US major accounts and targets, in accordance with agreed business objectives.

Key responsibilities:
1. Maintain and develop computerized customer and prospect database
2. Plan and carry out direct marketing activities to agreed budgets, sales volumes, values, product mix and timescales
3. Develop sales campaigns and create offers for direct mail and marketing to major accounts by main market sector and CV product range
4. Respond to and follow up sales enquiries by post, telephone, email and site visits
5. Maintain and develop existing and new customers, through active key account management and liaison with internal order-processing staff
6. Monitor and report on activities and provide relevant management information (MI)
7. Undertake market research, competitor and customer surveys
8. Maintain and report on equipment and software suitability for direct marketing and sales reporting purposes
9. Liaise and attend meetings with other company functions necessary to perform duties and aid business and organizational development
10. Manage the external marketing agency activities of telemarketing and research
11. Attend training and develop relevant knowledge and skills

Scale and territory indicators:
Core product range of 12 tool sets price range $80 to $450. Target sectors: All major multiple-site organizations having more than 500 personnel. Prospect database c.10,000 HQs of large organizations. Customer base of c.150 large organizations. Typical account value $20 to $50 p.a. Total personal revenue accountability potentially $4.5m p.a. Territory: USA

Under the CAREER acronym, there are a number of other words I could have used in R, including 'Replicable' or 'Repeatable'. The CV reviewer will be looking for indicators that the achievements, skills and experience referred to in your CV, as well as being relevant, can be repeated in the role for which you are applying. When an organization seeks an individual who is 'experienced in the role', what they are essentially saying is we want someone who has performed in this role before and can do so again at a competent level.

In order to pass this part of the CV sifting process, it is therefore critical that you:

- carefully read the job description and understand what types of skill and experience are required in the role
- match your relevant skills and experience in a way that specifically addresses the requirements of the role
- make it easy for the reviewer, who will be reading your CV at speed, to make the link between the requirements of the role and what you have to offer.

Seeking a second opinion

It is common practice in recruitment for a second opinion to be sought on CVs before the decision is made to invite a person to interview. In some cases, two individuals will work together to review all CVs. However, it is more common for one, usually junior, individual to undertake an initial review of CVs (removing those containing spelling errors as well as those that do not fit the job description), before passing on a much reduced pile of CVs to a manager or specialist who is normally closer to the role vacancy in question and who has a very clear idea of what is required.

It is also increasingly common for the initial phase of the recruitment process to be outsourced to a recruitment agency. In such instances, you have to negotiate this initial barrier before your CV gets in front of the final decision maker. Where you are aware that the types of role you intend to apply for are likely to pass through a recruitment agency as a first stage, you might find it productive to build a relationship with

SUNDAY

MONDAY

TUESDAY

WEDNESDAY

THURSDAY

FRIDAY

SATURDAY

those agencies preferred by your targeted employer. Again, undertaking some initial research will be likely to identify such agencies. Consider making approaches to them before a specific role becomes available and they may be quite helpful in terms of offering guidance on the suitability of your CV. If it is what they believe their clients are looking for, they may offer to submit your CV not only to the prospective employer you had in mind but for other positions that are not advertised in the open press.

Recruitment agencies tend to receive payment for their services from the employer, normally expressed as a percentage of your starting annual salary.

 Be wary of agencies that seek to charge you for their services.

Due diligence and cross-checking

The majority of checking and validation of what is contained in your CV and what you say at interview takes place through the referencing process once an offer of employment is made (the cost of checking all applicants in the early stages of the process would be too great). However, in instances where a CV is of particularly high quality and the reviewer wants some comfort that what is written has basis in fact, they may cross-reference your CV with the information about you that is available from social media sites and other sources before they meet you. Also, you should not underestimate the contacts that a reviewer may have within, and indeed outside, their sector. Such contacts might well know of you.

Whether you agree, or not, that social media sites or informal conversations should be used as a basis for determining your progression to the interview stage, these actions are a fact of life. As such, you should do what you can to manage your reputation across all sources, as far as possible.

TIP *Remember that it's not just a list of former jobs an employer is looking for; it's evidence that, as well as any role-specific requirements, you have certain core skills or attributes, such as good communication skills and self-awareness. Think about how you can articulate and demonstrate these.*

How organizations sift through CVs

Here is the list of the key steps that many organizations take in sifting through large volumes of CVs to identify the individuals that they really believe are equipped for the role or job position in question:

1 Glance over

2 Read through

3 Validating your CV against role requirements

4 Seeking a second opinion

5 Due diligence and cross-checking

Summary

For many people, taking time to focus on their own skills and experience and using these assets to construct a powerful CV seems to be an uncomfortable process. It is tempting to bundle elements together quickly, using a document you prepared in the past or even simply 'cutting and pasting' from a colleague's document or from an example you found online.

The reality of successful CV design is that it requires some work from you in digging down deep to reflect on your strengths and main areas of competence. It's not something that many people take to naturally, but seek opinions from others who you trust to be honest with you. This will give you additional insight into your strengths and weaknesses and will therefore be helpful in giving you a further perspective on the roles for which you are best suited.

From this secure position and clarity of purpose, you can build CVs to address any future roles of interest to you.

SUNDAY

MONDAY

TUESDAY

WEDNESDAY

THURSDAY

FRIDAY

SATURDAY

Fact-check (answers at the back)

The ten questions at the end of each chapter will help you to assess your understanding. Try to resist the temptation to look back through the chapter as you answer the questions. There is only one correct answer to each question. If you make a mistake, look back through the chapter and reread the section to help you understand the idea better.

Let's see how much you have picked up from our first day's thoughts on creating a successful CV.

1. The abbreviation CV:
a) Is a shortened version of Career Vector, meaning 'direction of career' ❏
b) Stands for the Latin phrase *curriculum vitae*, which translates as 'life path' ❏
c) Is short for Consultancy Vérité, meaning 'true consultancy' ❏
d) Was copyright protected by a recruitment agency in 1986 ❏

2. One of the primary purposes of a CV is to:
a) Give you something to talk about at the interview ❏
b) Manufacture a profile that the potential employer will find attractive ❏
c) Meet anti-discrimination legislation ❏
d) Demonstrate a strong match between your capabilities and the stated requirements of the role ❏

3. A small error in spelling or grammar in your CV:
a) Demonstrates in a positive way that you work at a fast pace ❏
b) Could lead to it being discarded in the initial 'glance through' ❏
c) Is of no consequence as the reviewer will focus on your obvious strengths ❏
d) Cannot be helped and is just one of these things ❏

4. Experience suggests that the percentage of CVs discarded at the first review stage is:
a) 50 per cent ❏
b) 90 per cent ❏
c) 25 per cent ❏
d) 10 per cent ❏

5. In the acronym CAREER, what does the A represent?
a) Artistic ❏
b) Altruistic ❏
c) Appropriate ❏
d) Authentic ❏

6. Getting hold of the relevant 'job description' or 'role profile' before constructing your CV is:
a) A waste of effort as it is purely your qualifications and experience that count ❏
b) Something that can be done only through a recruitment agency ❏
c) Essential, since it enables you to tailor your skills and experience to those required for the specific role ❏
d) Useful if you have the time to request and review it ❏

7. Demonstrating 'emotional intelligence' in your CV:
a) Can be an important differentiator as organizations are keen to employ individuals with good self-awareness and an ability to interact effectively with other people at all levels ☐
b) Is useful only where you are applying for positions in caring professions ☐
c) Is a sign of weakness ☐
d) Is impossible ☐

8. Use of the summarizing personal statement in a CV:
a) Is now totally discredited and should no longer be used ☐
b) When carefully constructed can provide a powerful, immediate and accurate understanding of your capabilities to the reviewer ☐
c) Is only used by people who lack genuine skills and experience ☐
d) Turns it into a legal document ☐

9. Leaving a gap in your employment history:
a) Is advisable if you have been unemployed or in prison during the period in question ☐
b) Should be avoided as it may lead to your CV being discarded without you being given an opportunity to explain ☐
c) Is so common during periods of economic downturn that it is no longer an issue ☐
d) Is a good ploy for getting an interview as the reviewer will be curious ☐

10. Once you have created your CV:
a) You may use it as a basis for constructing future role-specific CVs but be wary of using it unedited for other roles ☐
b) You can use the same document as often as you like as it contains the essential details of your skills and experience ☐
c) As you know it works, pass it on to your friends to use ☐
d) As you've used it once, you must destroy it immediately ☐

SUNDAY

MONDAY

TUESDAY

WEDNESDAY

THURSDAY

FRIDAY

SATURDAY

The core elements of a successful CV

Today we look in detail at the core components that make up a CV. We look at two main types of structure: the traditional approach and the 'achievement-based' approach.

Many organizations still have a preference for the traditional layout of CV, in which you list your personal and contact details, previous employments, educational qualifications and references – in that order. However, many applicants are finding success in restructuring their CV to convey their achievements in a way that is adapted and relevant to the role for which they are applying.

My view is that in following this second approach, you do not disadvantage yourself when presenting your CV to reviewers that prefer the traditional approach, while providing the opportunity to impress those organizations that prefer to see an achievement-based approach.

In examining the factors that will help you to construct your CV in a way that best represents your capabilities and suitability to the role you desire, we will look at a number of components:

- Structuring the content
- Personal statement
- Achievements
- Employment
- Education and qualifications
- References

Structuring the content

There is, as you will be aware, a huge body of work advising on how best to structure your CV. Success depends on a range of factors including the preferred style of the person reviewing your CV, the culture of the particular sector you are interested in and the process used by the organization offering the role in shortlisting CVs for the interview stage.

The primary focus of your CV should be to secure you a place at the interview stage. The best way of achieving this objective is to help the reviewer see as quickly as possible on starting to read your CV that your skills and experience match the requirements of the position on offer. In my opinion, simply listing your employments and qualifications in chronological order under the traditional approach is like setting out the ingredients of a recipe and leaving someone else to combine the various elements in the correct proportions and order. Alternatively, by ordering your skills and experience into the correct combinations to match the requirements of the new role, you are making it much easier for the reviewer to see the links between you and the role. This gives you an advantage over applicants of similar skills and experience who have not adapted their CV in such a way.

Tempting as it may be, you should not try to use your CV to answer all the questions a prospective employer may have about you as these can be addressed at the interview. Such an approach will make the document too long and could lead to it being discarded.

 Every statement you include in your CV should earn its place in linking your capabilities to the role. If it doesn't, take it out.

The key elements

In order to get that green light to the interview stage, it is vitally important that you get the key elements of your skills and achievements across to the reviewer as soon as possible (you will find out later why I recommend that in most instances you should restrict the length of your CV to two pages). Remember that a reviewer's impressions start to form as soon as they pick up your document.

In the past, conventional wisdom was that a CV should be arranged in this order:

- Personal details (name, address, etc., date of birth)
- Employment history (in reverse chronological order, i.e. most recent role first)
- Education (school, further or higher education)
- Other qualifications and skills (driving licence, languages, etc.)
- Hobbies and interests
- References (names and contact details, usually of two references)

The above structure is, and will continue to be, seen by many as the conventional way of documenting your personal details, skills and experience. Many employers still expect to see a layout similar to that described above.

In my view, however, this approach contains one big flaw. It leaves the effort involved in linking your capabilities to the requirements of the role to the person reviewing your CV. During periods when the ratio of CVs to vacancies is tens if not hundreds to one, such CVs, unfortunately, are likely to be discarded in the first review. Simply put, you have to do some of the hard work to relate your skills and experience to the new position, and not leave it all to the person reviewing your CV. More likely than not, a reviewer will not expend the effort, preferring instead to look in more detail at a CV that has already begun the process for them. After all, such CVs tend to indicate a person who has studied and understood the job description and has already started to put forward aspects of their skill and experience that relate directly to the specific role in question.

More recently, there has been a tendency towards structuring a CV in a way that communicates your relevance to the available position as quickly as possible, making reference to aspects of your skills and experience in ways that match the requirements of the role.

The structure favoured increasingly today, under the 'achievement-focused' approach, follows this order:

- Personal statement
- Achievements relevant to the new role
- Employment history – most recent first
- Education and qualifications
- Contact details and additional relevant personal information

The two main approaches to CV structure

There are two primary ways of structuring your CV:

Traditional

1 Personal/contact details

2 Employment history (most recent listed first)

3 Education/key qualifications

4 Other relevant qualifications and skills (e.g. driving licence)

5 Additional personal information

6 References

Achievement-focused

1 Personal statement

2 Achievements

3 Employment history (most recent listed first)

4 Education and qualifications

5 Contact details and relevant personal information

The achievement-focused approach helps the person reviewing your CV to quickly see the links between your capabilities and the requirements of the role. This is particularly important where your current position does not exactly match the one for which you are applying.

The personal statement

A relatively recent development is the personal or character statement I referred to earlier. While this element can have a very positive impact when used correctly, when not it can be seen as clichéd to the point that it is either ignored completely or becomes a point of amusement for the reviewer. I know of several organizations where the most outlandish and exaggerated of such statements are pinned on the wall. As such, I would advise that you carefully construct the statement that takes up this prominent space, seeking to inform the reader who you really are and how you can help their organization.

Let's explore the following contrasting examples to help get the point across. Which one would you prefer to read if you were reviewing CVs within a limited time frame?

Example 1

James is a dynamic, forward-thinking individual who grasps every opportunity open to him. He is a strong team player who is also known for his leadership qualities and is a true asset to any organization seeking to employ him. He is now ready to face his next big challenge.

Example 2

I am a qualified project manager with eight years' experience in the utilities sector, three of which were spent overseas. I have personally managed four projects with budgets in excess of $20 million, all of which completed on time and within budget.

I would hope that the question I asked before setting out these two examples was an easy one to answer. Before I dissect these very different approaches, just take a couple of minutes to compare them and note their differences. Which approach does your opening statement normally take?

It is worth investing time in your CV's initial statement since it is second only to the immediate appearance of your document (which we will cover later) in creating an impression on the reviewer. Bearing in mind, as we said earlier, that many reviewers take a matter of seconds to form an opinion, it is essential that your CV 'locks in' to what skills and experience the prospective organization seeks for the vacant role.

Let's now compare the two examples in detail to see if you picked up on the points I have in mind.

The two statements are of approximately the same length and therefore take up the same amount of space on the document. It is important that this initial paragraph is not too long. Interestingly, the first example runs to 50 words, whereas the second runs to 42 words. Lengthwise, I would say that both are acceptable.

Now, let's turn to the content of each of these statements. Which one gives the reviewer the most useful information at this earliest opportunity, in your opinion? You may argue that the first example is the most telling in that it gives insight into the applicant's character, determination and so on. I would agree that it is the most revealing, but not necessarily in a good way, and might lead to immediate discarding of the CV, and here is why:

- **It is too generic.** This first example could have been used in every CV sent out by our applicant James. It therefore fails one of the 'golden rules' of a successful CV, which is that it should be tailored to the position in question. Indeed, some commentators on this subject go as far as to suggest that a CV should be started from scratch for each and every new position for which you apply. In following this approach, you should therefore think carefully about what content goes in, and just as importantly, what content stays out. While I believe a CV should be tailored to each new job application, I do not think it necessary to start afresh each time, particularly if you have worded your achievements (which we will look at in more detail shortly) strongly. However, I do firmly believe that you should write a new and individually tailored initial or personal statement for each CV you submit.

- The first example speaks of James' personal qualities, yet provides no **context or example for such supposed personal strengths.** In comparison, the second example uses figures and timescales to indicate what level of activities the applicant has undertaken as well as their likely levels of seniority and responsibility (indicated by the size of budget they have managed). This approach tends to leave it to the reviewer to determine what qualities and skills a person has from a description of their achievements, rather than rely only on unsubstantiated claims made by the applicant themselves.

- This next point may be a personal bugbear of mine, but it is one that is mentioned by many reviewers I know. I refer to the **increasing tendency for people to refer to themselves in the third person** (James is a ...), when they have written the document themselves. Very few of us are in a position to have other people author their CVs for them and this is intended to be a document written by you and about you. There is absolutely nothing wrong in referring to yourself in the first person. Anything else is an unnecessary affectation.

To summarize on the personal statement, it should:

- relate directly to the role for which you are applying
- be no more than four lines / 50 words
- be written in the first person (I am...)
- contain specific, quantifiable information that is relevant to the role
- above all else, convey effectively why the reviewer should read further and consider you for interview, even after only having read your first 50 words or so.

It is a good idea to draft your personal statement when you start to build your CV and revisit it again once you have completed it, making any adjustments to ensure that the statement accurately reflects the main body of the document. This statement should strive to be a mini CV in itself, giving a true flavour of your distinguishing abilities and relevance to this specific role.

Achievements

After the personal statement, the next component to be added to your CV is a list of relevant achievements. This section of short paragraphs demonstrates succinctly to the reader that you have previously used your skills and experience to undertake aspects of the role for which you are now applying.

The technique is a simple yet highly effective one that assists the reviewer in connecting you with the role. It does involve you having a clear understanding of:

- the key components of your previous roles, such as:
  - key objectives and targets that you met
  - any budgetary responsibilities
  - any managerial responsibilities
  - how you approach planning
  - the degree of autonomy or freedom you had in your role
  - details of any improvements you made, how you influenced others, including your managers, to adopt your suggestions
- examples which demonstrate the above
- the primary requirements of the role for which you are applying, such as:
  - what similarities there are between your previous role and the new one

- where there are clear similarities in the types of skill and experience required
- where there are obvious connections between your achievements in previous roles and the requirements of the current role.

The key difference between the conventional method of setting out your CV and the achievement-based approach is in drawing out common aspects from your previous roles and applying them in a structured way to the new one. Imagine if you will that your career to date is like Rubik's Cube, the three-dimensional mechanical puzzle. When fully complete, each of this puzzle's solid coloured sides represents one of your various previous jobs. Under the traditional approach to describing your career to date, you would simply list each of these jobs in your CV one by one. However, under the achievement-based approach, it is as if you start to twist and rotate the various components of the cube, mixing up the small squares that made up each of the original sides. If you imagine that each job is made up of a series of elements, then you start to see the analogy. Each job is made up of a number of skills and sets of experiences that you can use to be successful in other roles, even if you have not undertaken that exact type of role previously.

You can take the Rubik's Cube analogy further, in that for some roles there are skills or traits that are not close to the surface in terms of their relevance for a particular role. However, slightly reconfigure the role and such skills might play a bigger part in its requirements, bringing about a change in emphasis in how you blend the description of your accumulated talents.

This approach can make you more confident in applying for jobs that do not, on the face of it, appear to be exactly the same as your previous roles. Start to see your previous roles as combinations of your various skill sets, which can be reconfigured and rebuilt to meet the demands of new roles. Never again see a job as a singular, set entity; instead see it as a combination of skills and capabilities, some of which you may be stronger in than others.

In adopting this approach, it is possible that you as an applicant might bring it to the attention of a prospective employer that their vacant position may benefit from certain skills or traits that they had not previously considered but which you possess.

Let's now look at examples of achievements and how to construct them. To remind you, the objectives of such paragraphs are to:

- capture examples of how your skills and experience have been applied to meet the objectives of your roles in the past
- lead the reviewer to conclude that such skills and experience can be applied to the new role.

Example 1
IT Migration Project: As IT programme leader, for 2 years from origination to completion, I led a successful €30 million project to migrate IT systems to a new platform. I reported directly to the main board and ran a core team of 15 project managers and 7 contract staff. All major milestones and budget targets were met.

Example 2
In-house sales training programme: As head of design on this project, I was responsible for the scoping and development of an 18-month duration sales programme for 400 sales representatives in three countries. A key part of my role was development of multicultural material acceptable to all territories. Feedback on the design component of the programme averaged 4.2 out of 5 with a 92 per cent response rate.

Example 3
Office relocation: Reporting directly to the CEO, I was responsible for the planning and execution of office relocation to a different city with a key objective of providing an uninterrupted service to clients. Critical aspects such as utilities, communications and personnel relocation / desk planning were under my direct control. Being able to plan and undertake this project internally saved the company $40,000 in external costs.

All these three examples of achievements included the following elements:

- Reference to the key objective or requirement
- The role of the applicant in the project
- Some indication of degree of responsibility – personnel or budget
- The outcome.

While the scale or size of each of the examples may vary, this is not important since it is the structuring of the content we are interested in. The use of different scales of budget are merely to indicate that the same structure can be used whether you are aiming for a board-level appointment or considering your first move upward in your career.

The reviewer is interested in how what you have achieved previously can be used for the benefit of their organization should you be appointed to the role. In each of the three examples, the applicant can be seen at the heart of the project.

Such an approach, if structured well, can convey key aspects applicable to many roles, including:

- a willingness to take responsibility and have experience in doing so
- experience in coming into contact with and managing day-to-day problems and issues
- experience of reporting progress to the next level of seniority and having an awareness of and experience in working to timescales and budgets
- a proactive and problem-solving approach to work, which can be picked up on by an experienced reviewer.

TIP *Using active words and phrases rather than passive ones tends to denote someone who prefers to shape their environment rather than let their environment shape them.*

It should go without saying that wording in a CV itself is no proof of a proactive and committed individual, since anyone can place these words on a piece of paper. An experienced interviewer will investigate statements made in a CV to determine their accuracy. The role of a CV, you will recall, is to get you through to the interview stage by highlighting your relevant skills and experience as clearly and succinctly as possible. It should not be used to make claims that cannot be supported at the interview stage.

What the CV can do, however, is show your skills and experience in the most effective combination to demonstrate their relevance to the position in which you are interested.

I hope that you can now see the advantage of adopting this achievement-based approach over the traditional approach of reciting your past roles and positions in reverse chronological order. The traditional approach, while easy to adopt and even easier to reproduce for future applications, requires no real hard work on your part and as such is more likely to fail in making strong links for the reviewer between your attributes and the vacant role.

So, let us now take a moment to consider what we have built into your new CV. We have drafted a personal summary statement (which we will fine-tune once the CV has been completed) and we have given examples of achievements, using the guidance above, to demonstrate our suitability for the role. You should order these achievements, aiming to give four or five, in the order of most relevant first. If you believe, for example, that sales and marketing experience and results are key to the new role, you should list this most relevant of your achievements first.

Employment history

Although you have used the Achievements section of your CV to demonstrate the relevance of the skills and experience you have gained from your current and previous role to the one for which you are applying, it remains helpful to the reviewer, and indeed is still expected, for you to list your recent employments.

Starting with your current employment first, you should include the following elements for each listing:

1 **Dates of joining and leaving that employment**
2 **Type of employer and sector**
3 **Your role – being specific but succinct**

Again, there is debate concerning exactly what else to include in this section of your CV. I will go through each of these elements, explaining the rationale for including them or leaving them out before offering you my opinion as to which approach you should take. Ultimately though, it is your decision, based on the specifics of your situation and any stated requirements from your prospective employer.

4 **Name of employer and your manager**

Many applicants decide to include the name and address of their employer in relation to each employment entry. Others go as far as to include the name of their department and the name of their manager. This has tended to be the traditional approach but it is my view that such information should be left out since it fails one of my tests for inclusion mentioned earlier. You may recall me saying that each statement included in your CV should earn its right to be there. I hold the view that while the role you undertook, the type of organization you were employed by and the length of your time there are relevant to an understanding of your capabilities, these additional details don't necessarily improve your case. Indeed, the experiences of the reviewer in relation to one of your former organizations, whether conscious or not, may have a negative impact on how they perceive your CV. Of course, any negative perceptions of one of your previous employers (or indeed a previous manager) will still exist if revealed at the interview stage but at least, by being present, you will have an opportunity at that stage to identify and manage such potential objections. At the initial CV stage, this obviously isn't possible and any reviewer prejudices will go unchallenged.

There is one exception I can think of in going against this reasoning. If you have been fortunate enough to have undergone training or a spent a period of time working for a respected market leader in the sector, then mentioning the name of such an organization in your CV could possibly provide you with an advantage over those who haven't. In this instance, rather than including the name in the Employment section, I would include it as part of your initial personal statement.

Remember that you are trying to create a positive impression as soon as possible in your CV: use your best material first.

Example
An Adams & Jones trained accountant, I have specialist experience of forensic risk management in the US investment banking sector....

5 Reason for leaving

Again, traditionally, this element is almost always included. However, I question the right of this particular piece of information to be in your CV. Can you think of any reason for leaving that would be responsible for making you attractive to a potential employer? In reality, although this element is normally included, the reasons usually given are clichéd, such as 'left to take up a more responsible position' or 'headhunted by a competitor'. As such, this information is seldom given any degree of attention by a CV reviewer, unless you provide a negative reason such as having been dismissed for gross misconduct. This raises the question as to whether you should disclose such unfortunate circumstances in your CV or whether it is acceptable to do so at interview.

The fundamental principle is that you should not be dishonest or misrepresent yourself; this means giving the correct response to questions you are asked on application forms, pre-interview questionnaires and at interviews. This is particularly relevant to questions around any criminal record, financial circumstances, and you being what's known as 'fit and proper' to undertake the role in question.

Be prepared to disclose any fact about yourself that is material to a prospective employer's decision about whether to employ you or not. The point I am making here is that including a reason for leaving such as not seeing 'eye to eye' with your previous manager, without giving yourself an opportunity to explain the background, could lead to your CV being discarded at the review stage, but be readily understood and accepted were it to be raised at the interview stage. On the other hand, an applicant involved in fraudulent activities applying for a role in a financial management capacity is unlikely to be accepted regardless of whether they disclose this issue at CV or the interview stage. (Remember, non-disclosure of material facts is likely grounds for instant dismissal months if not years after you are appointed, and will also seriously damage your future employability prospects.)

6 Salary

It is assumed that disclosure of your joining and leaving salaries at your previous employers are helpful to the new organization in seeing a rising figure, no doubt indicative of increasing responsibility. Again, I would question the benefit of automatically including your salary details in your CV.

The requisite combination of skills and experience should be the key factors in determining your suitability for the new position. For a whole range of reasons, it is possible that you might have been underpaid or overpaid in relation to your capabilities in the past; none of this is relevant to your current application. The new employer should have determined the market rate for the position in question and have made that figure known when advertising the role. If you believe you have the attributes to undertake the role set out by the employer in return for the specified remuneration, then your previous salary levels are an unnecessary distraction to the key equation.

7 Detailed job description for each role undertaken

The danger of detailing each and every role is two-fold:

- You increase the length of the document to the point that the reviewer discards it as being too long and repetitive.
- The key information the reviewer needs is obscured by this unnecessary additional wording.

As we will cover in further detail later, a successful CV manages to convey sufficient information on your relevant skills and experience to get you to first interview. It also creates 'hooks' or points of interest that an interviewer will wish to explore further. You can set up these signposts within your CV to point to areas you would like to discuss further at interview and which further reinforce your ability to fulfil the requirements of the new role.

Education and qualifications

Where a degree or other qualification is key to the role, again follow my general advice to present your best supporting material as soon as possible, including reference to these in your personal statement or achievements. The most effective way of doing this is by beginning one of your statements with this information, before continuing to describe a particular achievement.

Example
With a PhD in molecular sciences, I was responsible for running a team of 20 researchers working on a 4-year £3.5 million project to investigate the role of temperature fluctuation on hydrogen fuel cell depletion.

In the Education and qualifications section, it is normally sufficient to list your qualifications as follows, from the highest level downward:

- Higher degree (PhD, Masters, etc.) – institution and subject
- First degree – institution, subject and level of award
- Schooling – name of school or college and summary of type and number of qualifications obtained

It is unnecessary to provide details of your junior school. It is also unnecessary to detail every school qualification obtained; only include these if they are relevant (for example, a minimum qualification required in language or mathematically related subjects) or when specifically requested by the employer.

Contact details and additional personal information

Under this section, you should provide clear details of how you may be contacted, and include your:

- postal address
- email address
- contact telephone number.

You should provide brief details of any other relevant qualifications or experience in this section, such as language skills (your degree of fluency).

References

Unless they are specifically requested, I suggest you do not provide names and contact details of references. These are almost always only taken up just prior to, or even after, an offer of employment has been made. As such, these details are not normally required at the CV review stage.

Summary

You can significantly increase your chances of securing an interview if you can capture your suitability for a role in a well-structured, clear and brief CV. Today we have suggested a structure that can help you accomplish this objective. We have also suggested what types of information you can exclude from your CV, either because you can provide it at interview or because it is irrelevant in determining your suitability.

In putting your CV together, you should:

- be very clear from reading the job description what the person reviewing your CV is looking for
- aim to include the most relevant of your skills and experience first
- consider using the achievement-based approach to demonstrate your suitability
- make sure that each piece of information you include adds positively to your case
- resist the temptation to turn your CV into a chronological narrative of your career to date.

SUNDAY

MONDAY

TUESDAY

WEDNESDAY

THURSDAY

FRIDAY

SATURDAY

Fact-check (answers at the back)

1. A reviewer tends to form an impression of an applicant from their CV:
   a) Within seconds of having read the first few lines ❏
   b) By holding it up to a light ❏
   c) After approximately five minutes ❏
   d) After having read the complete document ❏

2. The most effective way of structuring your CV, according to this book, is:
   a) Contact details; employment history; education and qualifications; additional qualifications; references ❏
   b) Starting with your junior school details and continuing from then on a chronological basis ❏
   c) Personal statement; achievements; employment; education and qualifications; contact and other relevant personal information ❏
   d) By comprehensively listing your complete career history and educational achievements in reverse chronological order ❏

3. The objective of the initial personal statement is to:
   a) Introduce the CV reviewer to you as a person ❏
   b) Give the CV reviewer an understanding of your personality and other non-employment and qualification-related information ❏
   c) Inform the CV reviewer powerfully and succinctly why your skills and experience make you suitable for the vacant position ❏
   d) Fill in space on an otherwise sparse CV ❏

4. Ideally, the initial personal statement should contain this number of words:
   a) 10 ❏
   b) 50 ❏
   c) 250 ❏
   d) 1,000 ❏

5. The most effective type of achievement description should *not* include:
a) A specific example of how you have used your skills and experience to achieve a specific objective ☐
b) Hard information such as budgets, timescales, performance improvement percentages or return on investment ☐
c) Statements which cannot be supported by evidence when requested ☐
d) A proposal as to how previous experience makes you suitable for the new role ☐

6. What is the key advantage of the achievement-focused CV over the traditional approach?
a) It allows you to produce a longer CV ☐
b) It provides the reviewer with an accelerated understanding of how your skills and experience can be applied to the requirements of the new role ☐
c) It takes minimum effort to produce ☐
d) Traditionally structured CVs are now discarded at the very first stage ☐

7. Which of the following, in the author's opinion, should *not* be included in a CV, unless specifically requested:
a) Previous salary details ☐
b) Previous achievements ☐
c) Details of language skills ☐
d) A contact email address ☐

8. Your reason for leaving previous employments:
a) Should always be given in your CV, even if it reflects negatively on you ☐
b) Is not a key consideration for determining your suitability for selection for interview and as such should not be included in your CV unless specifically requested ☐
c) Is one of the most important factors in determining your suitability for a new role ☐
d) Should always be portrayed as someone else's fault ☐

9. Your salary in relation to previous employments:
a) Is not a relevant factor in determining your suitability for a new role and should not normally be included in your CV ☐
b) Should always be disclosed in your CV as this gives your potential new employer an idea of your 'market worth' ☐
c) Should be inflated as far as possible using bonuses and benefits in order to get the best chance of a high salary from the new role ☐
d) Must never be higher than the salary applying to the new role ☐

10. References should be included in your CV:
a) Only if requested by the prospective employer in their pre-application communications ☐
b) Never ☐
c) Always ☐
d) As a matter of pride ☐

SUNDAY

MONDAY

TUESDAY

WEDNESDAY

THURSDAY

FRIDAY

SATURDAY

TUESDAY

The 'look and feel' of a successful CV

Today we examine key elements of your CV such as the way it looks, as well as specific details of content and the impression these elements have on reviewers. We will look at the factors that make the best impression on reviewers, increasing your chances of passing to the next stage – the all-important interview.

A number of the elements covered in this chapter, such as correct spelling, apply to all CVs. For other elements such as whether to include a photograph of yourself or not, I give my opinion based on experience as to the best approach to take. In some countries, certain rules covered in employment law determine how an employer must conduct fair recruitment practices, such as not discriminating on the basis of age, gender, race, religion or other personal factors. While the responsibility lies with an employer to follow employment law, it would be useful for you as an applicant to have a basic understanding of what an employer is permitted to ask you about yourself under the employment and anti-discrimination laws applying in your country.

Let us now start to work through a range of issues that concern applicants and employers alike when it comes to deciding what makes a successful CV:

- Spelling and grammar
- Length
- Use of photographs
- Age and date of birth
- Physical construction of your CV
- Additional advice on CVs submitted via recruitment agencies

Spelling and grammar

I cannot underline enough the importance of correct spelling and grammar in your CV. It must be capable of passing the 'once over' glance of an eagle-eyed CV reviewer and in getting past the first cut. A decision to discard a CV can be made in as little as a couple of seconds.

If you are aware that spelling may not be your strongest skill, or even if you think it is, please use a spell checker and ask a family member or friend to read your document for spelling and correct grammar. Many organizations view spelling errors as grounds for dismissing CVs at the first hurdle on the basis that the individual has had ample opportunity to construct the document correctly. The view goes that if an individual cannot get their CV right, their attention to detail may be suspect and therefore insufficient for the role for which they are applying.

Length

A good piece of advice on the length of CVs is that they are rarely criticized for being too short but are often discarded for being too long. If you haven't received the green light to pass to the next stage by the end of your CV's second page, you are unlikely to have changed the reviewer's mind by the end of page seven, if they were to ever get that far.

The secret of an excellent CV is that it captures the reviewer's interest by two-thirds down the first page and uses the remainder of the document to support the reviewer's impression that you should be asked to attend for interview.

In my personal view, therefore, a CV should be no longer than two pages. Any longer and you increase the chances that the reviewer will become irritated or impatient with your document. My own preference, when I have been required to deliver a CV or resumé for a piece of work or project, is to restrict myself to one single side of one sheet. My success rate with this technique, interestingly, is in excess of 90 per cent.

SUNDAY

MONDAY

TUESDAY

WEDNESDAY

THURSDAY

FRIDAY

SATURDAY

There are exceptions to this approach, where further detail on an applicant is required at this initial stage. For example, a medical doctor applying for a post with a different health authority in another region may need to provide a detailed list of qualifications, experience and skills that run to several more pages than the length recommended here. However, I think it is safe to say that those applying for such roles will be aware of the conventions applying to their particular sector. For the majority of roles, it is possible, and indeed desirable, to match your key achievements to the requirements of the new role within two pages.

Use of photographs

You should not normally include a photograph with your CV unless asked specifically to do so (perhaps if you are a model or actor where physical appearance is an element of the selection process). In many parts of the world there is specific anti-discriminatory or equal opportunities legislation that prevents an employer from discriminating against an applicant on the grounds of race, religion, gender, sexual orientation, political beliefs, disability or age. While most employers operate within such rules, the inclusion of your photograph may subconsciously influence an individual reviewer (who perhaps through unconscious bias may prefer to recruit people who look similar to them). It is therefore generally recommended that you leave your skills and experience to represent you rather than include a photograph. The caveat to this point is that in some parts of the world, the inclusion of a photograph with a resumé is expected and part of normal practice.

In practical terms, many employers and recruitment agencies will remove photographs attached to CVs prior to review because of the potential discrimination issue or because they simply get in the way of copying and storing the CVs. Some potential employers may even discard a CV containing a photograph as soon as it is noticed to remove any possibility that they might be accused of discriminatory practices. As we will see in a later chapter, increasing numbers of employers and recruitment agencies now ask for CVs to be submitted to them in electronic format. The inclusion of a photograph can increase the size of an electronic file significantly and may even lead to the rejection of the file by the intended recipient's firewall or email scanning software which blocks images.

It is true that in an increasingly social media focused world there will be images of you available to a potential employer and that these may be reviewed informally as part of the recruitment process. However, in taking that approach, an employer carries the risk of mistakenly retrieving the image of a person with the same name as you (this has happened), and therefore this would not be normal practice for an employer or recruitment agency that follows correct procedures.

Age and date of birth

The inclusion of an applicant's age, date of birth or both of these items was once common in the traditionally structured CV. It was usually the second piece of information to be included after an applicant's name. Again, the impact of anti-discrimination legislation in many territories has led to a decrease in the inclusion of this biographical information in the initial CV document. Many territories have specific anti-discrimination legislation regarding age, with it being illegal to take into account someone's age in determining their ability to fulfil the requirements of the role in question.

Again, there is continuing debate around how effective the removal of any age-related data from your CV will be in preventing a reviewer from estimating your age. It is argued that they can do this simply by looking at the length of your career or in calculating from such details such as the year you obtained your degree or graduated from high school. While this may be true, this argument misses a key point that, in most territories, the whole direction of employment procedures has changed to incorporate anti-discriminatory practices.

Therefore, many employers, Human Resource departments and recruitment agencies no longer expect you to include reference to age, and indeed even gender, in your CV application. When you do, unless asked specifically to do so, you are potentially causing your prospective employer a dilemma.

TIP *Including your age on your CV at best may be ignored but at worst could actually lead to discarding of your CV as the reviewer may have some preconceived idea about the age range of the candidates they are seeking.*

Age and its relationship to a person's ability to perform a role remains a 'hot topic'. Let's look at the issue from a number of perspectives and in doing so examine how best to manage it in your CV.

People at the younger end of the spectrum might be concerned that their lack of years in the employment market may go against them. Conversely, those who have many decades of work behind them may feel that they will be seen as 'too old', 'tired' or have other negative connotations around their chronological age. My solution to dealing with this potential stumbling block to your career development, which may be due as much to your own mindset as any bias of a potential employer, is to focus on your achievements.

Within the consultancy work I currently undertake for many organizations of all different sizes and sectors across the world, I am extremely privileged to have met extraordinarily talented people with fantastic skills and experience, any one of whom it would be an honour to have working beside me. To give you a taster, these include:

- an individual who due to the unfortunate premature death of their father inherited a chain of 25 grocery stores, and despite having no previous experience in retail or commerce, has gained the trust of both customers and staff – turnover and profitability continue to grow
- a poet with incredible insights into the human condition and a fantastic presence; someone who has performed at the White House for the President of the United States
- a gifted linguist and much in demand management trainer who has written numerous articles on a wide range of subjects and can play almost any musical instrument, including 18 different stringed instruments
- a gifted pianist who plays the most beautiful Beethoven, having conquered the difficulties of coming from a war-torn nation to become a professional musician.

Even in such short descriptions, I would hope that my words convey the talents of these people. You will obviously have noted that in no instance did I make reference to age, gender, race or religious beliefs. Such factors are simply irrelevant to a person's abilities to perform a role.

There is an old saying in recruiting about whether a person has 20 years' experience or one year's experience repeated 20 times. In other words, the age of a person is not a reliable indicator of the experience or skills of that person and should not therefore be seen as a basis for making such a judgement. I have encountered many people, young and older, who have managed to build an impressive range of skills and experience into their career. Equally, I have also encountered people of all ages who, even despite opportunities being open to them, have not fulfilled their potential or even come close to doing so. You should not use your age as either a reason or an excuse for not having done something, as potential employers will always be able to point to someone of a similar age who will have managed such achievements.

TIP *Remove your age from your mindset and it will not be an issue for your potential employer.*

Physical construction of your CV

Let's now spend some time looking at the basic presentation elements of a physical (as opposed to an electronic) CV.

Type of paper

The standard advice is to use good-quality white paper. Some writers on the subject even advise the use of a particular weight of paper. In reality, your original CV is photocopied many times or even scanned by the organization reviewing your application, so the key is to make the job of doing so as easy as possible.

Do not used coloured paper, since this can make copies or electronic scans of your document difficult to read. Additionally, this is seen as a gimmick and does not lead to your CV being viewed as preferable to that of anyone else's in the pile. In fact, the person responsible for initially administering the arriving CVs may even photocopy it on to white paper to make it uniform with the others.

Binding or securing your CV

For similar reasons of practicality, do not invest time or money in binding or placing your CV in a booklet format. Remember, your CV document should be in the region of only two pages in length and should be held together with one staple. Any additional binding or stapling simply makes the likely task of duplicating your CV for multiple circulation that much more difficult. Again, think about ways of reducing any barriers that get between your CV and the relevant decision maker.

Spacing and formatting

The aim in formatting is to make your CV as readable and easy on the eye as possible. Do everything you can to make the reviewer focus on the content of your CV. Refrain from using page borders or other unnecessary embellishments which take away from the impact of your content. The best formatted and presented CVs are the ones where the reviewer doesn't notice these elements. I would also suggest that you print your pages on a single-sided basis, not double-sided, making it easier for your document to be copied. This may not appear environmentally sound but remember that my advice is that your CV is restricted to two pages.

CV presentation

- Make your CV easy to read using Times New Roman or Arial size 11 or 12 in black.
- Use plenty of white space.
- Keep statements short, using bullet points where possible.
- Try to keep to a maximum of two pages.
- Print on only one side of the paper.
- Use white not coloured paper.
- Check your spelling and check it again.

Font

It is tempting when following advice to keep a CV brief to try to squeeze in more information by reducing font size. Do not give in to temptation and remember that quality and relevance of content is much more important than quantity. Aim generally for an 11 or 12 point font size and stay with either Times New Roman or Arial. Avoid scripted (handwriting simulated) fonts at all costs as these can be difficult to read, especially for a reviewer who has been looking through CVs for several hours. A CV that is difficult to read may just require too much effort, regardless of the calibre of the applicant, and the CV will be discarded.

SUNDAY
MONDAY
TUESDAY
WEDNESDAY
THURSDAY
FRIDAY
SATURDAY

Use of imagery

As well as incorporating a portrait photograph of themselves, some candidates also include further imagery of them undertaking various roles or tasks. Again, it is neither necessary nor advisable to include such images in a CV for the vast majority of job applications. This advice has as much to do with the practicalities of copying or scanning your document as it does about the minimal effect it has on someone selecting your CV for the next stage.

CVs submitted via recruitment agencies

All of the above guidance applies when you make a direct application to the organization offering the role. In cases where you are invited to make your application through a recruitment agency, bear in mind that they may copy and place your CV on to their own stationery for submission to their client organization. Such stationery may contain the recruitment agency's logo and contact details, so again leave good space around the margins of your original document to enable them to do this easily.

Agencies will also tend to ask you to submit a version of your CV electronically. Some people prefer to do so in PDF (portable document format, designed by Adobe Systems) in order to protect formatting and presentation of their material. However, as mentioned above, some agencies prefer to transfer your details on to their own format or stationery, which is difficult to do with PDF files. You may therefore decide to send your electronic version of your CV in a Word document format, so that the agency may reformat it to fit the available space on their document. It would be useful for you to ask them about their preference before sending it to them.

Summary

Having put a great deal of thought into the content and structuring of your CV, it would be unfortunate if it were to be discarded on the basis of a presentational issue. Sadly, however, this can often happen where a CV reviewer spots a spelling error or simply finds it takes too much effort to read your CV because of the way it is set out. To put it bluntly, even if you are genuinely the most skilled and experienced person for the role, a badly designed CV may mean that you never get the chance to prove this at interview.

A range of presentational aspects, if not undertaken correctly, can damage your chances of proceeding any further than the initial review of CVs. Such elements include:

- the length of your CV – being too long can be an issue
- spelling or grammar mistakes
- poor formatting – poor use of white space or a cramped feel to the document
- use of coloured paper or coloured ink
- including unnecessary photographs or images.

Fact-check (answers at the back)

1. The presentation and look of your CV:
   a) Says much about your personality and individuality. As such, original approaches are recommended
   b) Is unimportant so long as you have the right skills and experience
   c) Should be your primary area of focus
   d) Should be structured so that it is the content that the reviewer focuses on, without any distractions

2. The length of a CV:
   a) Is directly proportionate to your skills and experience. As such, the longer your CV, the more likely it is that you will be selected for interview
   b) Is inversely proportional to the intelligence of the applicant
   c) Should be kept to a maximum of two pages in most cases
   d) Is unimportant – it is as long as it needs to be to get your point across

3. Correct spelling and grammar:
   a) Is so 'yesterday's news'
   b) Is vitally important in creating the right image for your CV
   c) Is unimportant so long as you have the right skills and experience
   d) Is only really important if you are intending to become a writer or journalist

4. The most effective font is:
   a) Whichever one the potential employer uses most in its own material
   b) Black, point size 11 or 12 in Times New Roman or Arial
   c) One of the handwriting-based scripts that helps to personalize your CV
   d) One that makes the most striking impression, leading the reviewer to pick your document from the pile

5. You should include a photograph of yourself:
   a) Undertaking one of your specialist roles as this proves and supports what you state in your CV
   b) Only if you are under 30 years old
   c) In all CV submissions as this helps the CV reviewer build up a better picture of your suitability
   d) Only when specifically asked to do so

6. You should submit hard copy versions of your CV that are:
   a) Printed on both sides as this is environmentally friendly
   b) Printed on one side only as this is generally easier to read and to photocopy where required
   c) Printed on both sides if the length of your CV exceeds four pages
   d) Printed on only the finest-quality paper

7. You should include details of your age or date of birth:
a) At all times, as many roles are best undertaken by people of a certain age ❏
b) Only when specifically asked to do so ❏
c) Because employers need to ensure that they don't pay younger people higher salaries than is necessary ❏
d) To help employers meet any anti-discrimination targets ❏

8. Applying binding to your CV or placing it in a folder:
a) Is unnecessary since most reviewers will remove such covers to enable copying or to file in their own system (electronic or hard copy) ❏
b) Is a fantastic idea as it makes your CV stand out above the rest in the pile ❏
c) Is the new trend ❏
d) Expresses your individuality and will be a key factor in selection for the next stage ❏

9. Electronically submitted CVs:
a) Should always be submitted in PDF format to maintain their structure and to prevent them being altered ❏
b) Can be submitted in a range of formats. It is advisable to ask the recipient in advance which format they prefer ❏
c) Should be avoided in all cases ❏
d) Demonstrate your IT skills and give you a real advantage over people who only submit hard copies ❏

10. When submitting an electronic version of your CV to a recruitment agency:
a) Be aware that they may wish to adapt it to fit within their own format before submitting to a potential employer. A Word document format may be best in such cases ❏
b) You give up your rights to anonymity ❏
c) You should ignore all the guidance related to paper copies ❏
d) You increase your chances of being selected ❏

WEDNESDAY

Knowing your way around your own CV

The main aim of your CV is to help you pass through to the interview stage of the selection process. However, having achieved this goal, its role is not yet complete since the document itself will often be used by an interviewer to determine what questions they may ask you at the interview itself.

Today we will look at the ways in which your CV can help you at the interview stage and how best to construct your CV to help you perform to your potential at a selection interview.

I do not intend to stray into interviewing techniques any further than is necessary to explain to you how a well-constructed CV can play an important role in a successful interview. We will look at such techniques as:

- 'hooks and trails'
- embedding key words and phrases
- critical incident interviewing techniques.

The CV and the interview

In preparation for an interview, a fully prepared interviewer will have gone through your CV, comparing its contents with the job description for the role in question. A key aim of theirs will be to assess your suitability and 'fit' against the roles and requirements of the position. To be successful, you should aim to make their task as easy as possible when it comes to your CV.

There still remain a small number of interviewers who ignore the CV once the interview stage has been reached. They prefer, instead, to use their 'gut instinct' to determine your suitability. Fortunately, these types are becoming less common and it is vitally important that you are able to navigate your way around your own CV competently and confidently, knowing where you can expand on material covered in your CV. (It should go without saying that a person who does not know their way around their own CV at interview will fail to impress.)

'Hooks and trails'

As you put together each element of your CV, in particular your personal statement and achievements, you should ask yourself the types of question an interviewer may ask you, based on the statements you make in your CV.

Definitions

Hook: 'A curved or sharply bent device, used to catch, drag, suspend or fasten something else'

Trail: 'A mark or a series of signs or objects left behind by the passage of someone or something'

Wherever possible, your statements should lead the interviewer to ask a question that gives you an opportunity to further demonstrate the fit between your skills and experience and the requirements of the role.

As we have said earlier, the CV is not intended to be an exhaustive and comprehensive record of your career and educational history to date. Each statement you include in your CV should indicate to the reviewer that you meet the requirements for the role. The information contained within each statement should reassure the reviewer that you have the necessary skill set and experience and lead them to a question that digs deeper into your suitability around that particular point. When such a question is asked, that is your cue to provide more detail on an achievement contained in your CV or to provide a further relevant example of an achievement that supports your suitability for that particular aspect. A request for more details or further examples as a result of statements contained in your CV should not come as a surprise to you. Be prepared with further examples and details.

In framing statements to go into your CV, think how you would answer questions such as:

● Tell me more about the work you did at...
● What particular challenges did you face in this role?
● I see that you regularly met your annual targets. What planning did you undertake each quarter to make this possible?
● How did you get into the position where you were responsible for a budget of £5 million?
● What are the main challenges in managing a 30-strong sales team?

Interviewers will use a range of open questions such as these examples. It will add to your chances of success if you are able to relate such questions back to key statements made in your CV, while being able to expand on them further.

Using the TED technique

One technique you can use to strengthen your CV and to increase your ability to navigate confidently around it is to ask a friend or family member to run the 'TED' exercise with you on your CV. 'TED' is a well-known questioning technique – you may have heard of it – which encourages a person to expand on statements they have already made, using this acronym which stands for Tell, Explain or Describe:

● **T**ell me more about...
● **E**xplain how you...
● **D**escribe an occasion where you...

Using your draft CV as the basis for discussion, your friend should review your CV (as of course they should be doing anyway to look for any spelling or grammatical errors) and then pick out a number of statements you have made. They should then use a number of the TED prompts to get you to expand more on those particular statements.

In following this technique, you can use your CV as the core of your approach, around which you build a series of additional examples to help support your application. These examples, which I again suggest are structured in the form of achievements, can be put together at the same time as your CV but not included within it. Instead, the use of key words or reference to such experience within your CV (i.e. the hooks and trails I refer to) will normally lead to an opportunity within the interview to use such examples. The alternative is to wait until the interview before thinking about forming such examples; not an approach I would recommend, particularly if you are also looking to demonstrate your planning and preparation capabilities.

Using the SMART technique

In Monday's chapter, we looked at how to structure an achievement and how this approach was more likely to connect your capabilities to the requirements of the role than just a straightforward description of your employment activities to date. Although more commonly thought of as means of setting goals and objectives, you might wish to use this (slightly adapted) SMART acronym to structure your achievement examples.

To do this, draft and then test each achievement example against the following adapted SMART acronym:

- **S**pecific: make your example specific to a particular requirement of the role for which you are applying. Identify this requirement from the job description.
- **M**easurable: include figures such as budgets, cost savings and percentage increase in sales/profitability to quantify your achievement.
- **A**chieved: in this context, make it clear what the achievement was and how it can be related to the new role. Address why the stated achievement demonstrates your suitability for the new role.
- **R**elevant: are you able to verify the achievement you describe as well as your central role in it? Achievements that you

observed 'from the touchline' but which cannot be linked to your actions, decision-making or involvement cannot be realistically used to demonstrate your impact on the new role.

- **T**imescale: include the time period within which your particular achievement was attained. This could be the duration of the project or the period over which you built the sales team or managed the cost reductions.

Embedding key words and phrases

As we have seen, 'hooks and trails' are intended to act as signposts within the CV leading to additional achievements or examples that you have constructed and can refer to at the interview stage.

The embedding of words or phrases of a particular type in your CV is intended to indicate to the reviewer particular characteristics that you wish to convey. For example, many employers are understandably keen to discover to what degree the achievements you describe in your CV can be attributed to your actions rather than to the input of others. To reinforce the idea that achievements were due largely to your own efforts, it helps your case if you are able to demonstrate your familiarity with key technical terminology or milestones. Such references should be used sparingly but if used in context can add plausibility to your submission.

Some employers are interested in any indicators that an applicant is proactive in shaping their own career and in having a problem-solving mindset. The inclusion of such words, sparingly, in your CV can start to reinforce that impression. Again, I remind you of my caveat that you should not seek to mislead within your CV. However, if you have been responsible for a particular achievement, it may be advantageous to use action verbs rather than document the achievement in a neutral or passive way (false modesty may not get your CV through).

Example 1 (passive)
The $10 million project in which I was involved was completed successfully two months before the due completion date.

Example 2 (proactive)
I played a significant planning role in the $10 million project, which was successfully completed two months before the due completion date.

Attention to the tense of verbs used by applicants is another indicator that reviewers sometimes use. This may sound a surprising approach but it is not uncommon for applicants to speak of what they would do in a certain situation, using future ('I will') or future conditional ('If this happened I would...') tenses, and for it to become evident subsequently that they had no experience in the area of interest. Consistent use of the past tense in a CV suggests that an applicant is used to describing events that have already occurred, and therefore that they have experience in that area.

Critical incident interviewing techniques

As well as determining whether your skills and experience are relevant to the role in question, potential employers are also subtly trying to find out more about you as a person and how you operate in different situations. You might think that this analysis takes place only from the interview stage. However, many organizations, and their appointed recruitment agencies, look for initial clues in your CV. Again, you should think about how you can leave hooks or trails that refer to such required qualities within your CV.

Many employers use the critical incident interviewing technique as part of the employment selection process. Essentially, at interview you are asked to think back to a situation you have been involved in and to describe how particular aspects such as people, decision-making process, risk management and budget as well as the problem itself were managed.

Prior to the interview stage, the employer will have identified a set of competencies that are central to the role for which you applied. At the interview itself, you will be scored against such competencies depending on your description of how the situation was handled and your role in such a situation. Again, this subject is best explored more fully under interview techniques but I raise it here as there are steps you can take when creating your CV to prepare for dealing with such a technique at the interview stage.

The person reviewing the CVs at the initial stage should be very familiar with the contents of the job description relating to the position in question. Additionally, they may also be aware of the detailed competencies the employer believes are required by the person best suited to fill that role. (These detailed competency requirements are sometimes, but not always, made known to applicants at the start of the process.) Therefore, in sifting through CVs at the first stage, the reviewer will already be starting to match what is seen on CVs against specific competency requirements that might not always be obvious to the applicant.

Not only does the achievement-based approach described earlier increase your chances of matching your profile to the requirements of the new role but the actual words or phrases you use may also positively influence the reviewer to select your CV from the tens or even hundreds spread out in front of them.

Many organizations work to the premise that a person who consistently behaved in certain ways in the past is likely to behave in similar ways in the future, i.e. when employed by them. An employer is therefore interested in identifying particular traits, or patterns of behaviour, that are appropriate to the new role. By wording your CV in a certain way, you can start to indicate to the prospective new employer that you have one or more of these desired attributes.

From your CV, indicators of particular types of trait, such as extroversion, receptivity to change or need for affiliation, can start to give an employer some early impressions as to the type of person standing behind the CV. For example, a CV with many job changes in a short period of time might indicate a person who becomes unsettled or easily bored in a role after a relatively short time.

> ## Definition
>
> Trait: 'A distinguishing feature, as of a person's character'
>
> 'A component of a person's behaviour that is assumed to serve as an explanation of enduring personal characteristics'

The messages you give out from your CV can therefore be quite subtle and, indeed, subconscious on your part. For this reason, I suggest that you review your drafted CV from yet another angle to discover what other messages it might give out to a potential employer. Having reviewed the requirements of the job description, your CV may indicate that you possess the following attributes that might be seen as desirable by a prospective employer:

- an ability to plan and organize yourself and others
- a willingness to work on your own or as part of a team as necessary
- an ability to make sound decisions based on the information available
- an ability to communicate with people at all levels around you
- a tendency to see a job through to completion.

The way in which you structure your statements can give the reviewer a significant amount of information regarding such attributes. Please note the major distinction between simply stating that you possess characteristics such as those described above and providing details of achievements that indicate you possess such characteristics. The former approach is unlikely to be taken at face value while the latter will be seen as a good starting point.

Think of the approach I am suggesting here as using your CV as a highly effective set of signposts. You give the CV reviewer sufficient range and depth of information to reassure them that you meet the requirements for the role but leave sufficient room to develop the various themes at your interview with further information. In addition, the way that you construct your statements gives the reviewer an indication of the types of personality traits you may have, which in turn will provide guidance as to the type of roles to which you are best suited, or unsuited, as the case may be. In reviewing your draft CV, you should identify and be comfortable with the messages about you that your CV sends out.

Reflect on what impresses you about other people and use this insight to bring out your own best qualities in your CV.

Using your CV as a navigation aid

Your CV is not meant to be a meandering narrative of your life story to date. It is a series of signposts that strongly direct the reviewer to the conclusion that you are right for the job. Since the reviewer may wish to explore some of the subjects you mention at interview, be clear on where your directions lead and what you need to cover if taken there.

Summary

Today we have learned that a CV does not only convey information concerning your skills and experience. The way you set out your CV and the words you use can provide a potential employer with useful indicators as to your personality type, the types of role you appear to prefer and how you react to different situations. While such information is not comprehensive, it is part of the picture an employer builds up to determine your fit with the role for which you have applied. It is therefore extremely important that you understand what additional indicators your CV provides to your potential new employer and how you make best use of such indicators.

We also looked at how you can embed particular words or phrases in your CV to act as signposts to further discussions at the interview stage. These hooks or trails that you lay down should invite the interviewer to further investigate the areas you suggest. Of course, in adopting this strategy, it is important that you invest time prior to interview in constructing such additional achievement-focused examples.

SUNDAY

MONDAY

TUESDAY

WEDNESDAY

THURSDAY

FRIDAY

SATURDAY

Fact-check (answers at the back)

1. Wherever possible, the statements contained in your CV should:
   a) Make you sound as important as possible ❑
   b) Prevent the interviewer from having any need to ask further questions about your application ❑
   c) Rhyme ❑
   d) Lead the interviewer to ask questions that give you an opportunity to further demonstrate the fit between your skills and experience and the requirements of the role ❑

2. The aim of a 'hook' in your CV is to:
   a) Create a point of interest that can be opened up to provide further related information at the interview stage ❑
   b) Distract the reviewer from weak areas of your CV ❑
   c) Trick the interviewer ❑
   d) Remind you of areas on which you should ask questions at the interview ❑

3. The achievements you include within your CV:
   a) Should be a mix of those you are responsible for and those you could have achieved had conditions been in your favour at the time ❑
   b) Should be the most relevant and should also be supported with others you have available to you, should you reach interview ❑
   c) Should act as teasers to the reviewer with you saving your best examples to reveal at interview ❑
   d) Do not have to be genuine so long as they appear convincing, as no one ever checks ❑

4. A trait is:
   a) Some type of reward ❑
   b) A type of experience ❑
   c) A distinguishing feature of a person's character ❑
   d) A type of personality ❑

5. The 'T' in the acronym TED stands for:
   a) Trust ❑
   b) Tell ❑
   c) Topic ❑
   d) Team ❑

6. The 'E' in the acronym TED stands for:
   a) Explain ❑
   b) Expert ❑
   c) Entertain ❑
   d) Experience ❑

7. The 'D' in the acronym TED stands for:
   a) Describe ☐
   b) Document ☐
   c) Detail ☐
   d) Discuss ☐

8. The regular use of the past tense in your CV:
   a) Suggests to the reader that you live in the past and are therefore unlikely to be suited to a newly created role ☐
   b) Is indicative, but not conclusive, that you have been involved in the situations you describe in your CV ☐
   c) Means nothing whatsoever and should be ignored ☐
   d) Suggests you have just used an old CV ☐

9. Critical incident technique interviewing:
   a) Is now totally discredited and should no longer be used ☐
   b) Is designed to ascertain how you did or might act in particular situations or scenarios ☐
   c) Is the term used for a particularly poor interviewing style ☐
   d) Is used only for roles in which risk management plays a key part ☐

10. A CV with several job changes in a short period of time might indicate:
    a) A person who becomes unsettled or easily bored in a role after a relatively short time ☐
    b) An ambitious person who hasn't yet found the role that challenges or fulfils them ☐
    c) A sector that is economically unstable with poor job security ☐
    d) All of the above plus other reasons, so conclusions should be drawn with caution and supported by other evidence ☐

SUNDAY MONDAY TUESDAY WEDNESDAY THURSDAY FRIDAY SATURDAY

THURSDAY

Other sources of information employers use

Today we highlight and consider other tools at the disposal of employers and recruitment agencies as they seek as much information as possible regarding your suitability for the position for which you applied. We devote a complete chapter (Friday) to the online world and its increasing impact on the application process.

Where once the CV was the main, if not only, pre-interview source of information open to employers in determining suitability for a role, this situation is changing rapidly. A successful applicant therefore not only needs to consider what goes into their CV but also how to reconcile what appears in their CV with what a prospective employer can discover from other sources of information.

Inconsistency is one factor that tends to set alarm bells ringing for an employer when seeking applicants for a vacant position. You therefore need to be informed and proactive in managing what the spectrum of sources indicates to your potential employer.

The other sources of information we will consider today are:

● the employer application form
● the personality or behaviour profiling test
● the 'fit and proper' questionnaire
● the handwritten covering letter.

The employer application form

Even if you are invited to submit a CV, a potential employer may also ask you to complete and return their application forms at the same time. This could be a hard copy but increasingly the online equivalent is being used. There is no evidence yet of widespread use of online analytics to observe the behaviours of a potential applicant's visit to the recruitment section of an organization's website. It may only be a matter of time, however, since the technology is already used elsewhere, before details are noted of which parts of the employer's site an applicant visited and how long they stayed, with this information used to add to the overall profile of the applicant.

Why organizations like application forms

In asking you to complete an application form, the organization is able to maintain some structure over the type of information you provide, more so than if it relied wholly on your CV, the contents of which are largely within your control. The information you provide is therefore likely to be more closely aligned to the information required by the employer since you will be guided by the headlines and questions in each section of the form.

Some application forms contain a declaration that the applicant is asked to sign, on the basis that the information provided may be more accurate and the applicant less inclined to exaggerate their skills and experience.

The application form may ask for information that is of more use to the organization were you to be eventually employed by them, such as your national insurance or social security number, date of birth and tax details. None of this information should be used in any way to determine your suitability for the role for which you have applied. Indeed, due to the anti-discriminatory legislation in place in many territories, requests for this and other types of personal information are now kept completely separate from the recruitment process so the organization can protect itself from any accusation of anti-discriminatory practices.

Additionally, you may be asked to complete a separate form asking for personal information such as your ethnic origin, whether you have any disabilities or your sexual orientation. Such a form is required in some territories as employers are legally obliged to maintain statistics as to the numbers of people they employ in particular categories, and this data is retained on an anonymous basis. Again, such information should play no part in determining your suitability for a role.

The personality or behaviour profiling test

Profiling tests are increasingly used to gain a richer picture of aspects of an applicant's profile such as:

- their preferred communication style
- whether they prefer to work on their own, in small groups or as part of a larger team
- whether they prefer roles that are well defined with tight parameters or whether they prefer more open-ended and less structured roles
- their tendency to complete tasks at a structured rate during the timeline available, or whether they tend to leave the bulk of the task until the last available opportunity.

These are only a few examples of some of the elements that such profiling can detect. On the whole, these tests are very well developed and consistently reliable in their findings. It is fairly difficult to deceive these profiling tools, and there is little point in doing so since their main aim is to align your personality and characteristics with a position that requires such a profile. If you end up in a position that requires you to behave in a way that is not aligned to your natural state, this will simply cause you stress, probably on a cumulative basis, leading to a likely move away from the role.

TIP *Always answer the questions related to these profiling tools as honestly as you can, because they can be very helpful to you in finding a role that fits your strengths.*

Possessed with the results of such a profiling test, which is usually shared with the applicant these days (ask for a copy), together with your CV, the recruiting organization is able to build a fairly accurate picture of the applicant. If you have undertaken a profiling exercise in the past, use the information gained from this source to inform and shape the messages arising from your CV to make them consistent.

Using profiling to enhance your CV

Personality profiling is becoming more common today as organizations keen to reduce staff turnover look more closely at the alignment between personality and approach to working and the role itself. Such increased understanding is not the sole domain of the employing organization: individuals can use profiling to identify how their strengths are better suited to some roles than others. Profiling tests are commonly available, most of them online. For guidance on which profiling test is best suited to your requirements, contact a local careers advice body or, alternatively, a reputable recruitment agency may be able to assist.

The 'fit and proper' questionnaire

You may already have encountered such a document if you are involved in any role that involves having access to an organization's financial affairs, are in a position where you have the capacity to contract on behalf of the organization that employs you, or a number of other instances where it is important for an organization prior to employing you to know that you meet what is generally known as 'fit and proper' standards. This means that you are required to declare specific aspects of your personal situation such as:

- a criminal record (different regulations apply in different territories as to what severity of conviction and as to whether 'time barring' can be applied after a certain period)
- your credit rating and levels of debt
- whether you are, or have been, declared insolvent or bankrupt
- whether you have ever been disqualified from holding the role of director or other senior position in an organization.

Again, the best approach to take with such a document is to answer it truthfully and honestly. In the event of an employment offer, the subsequent discovery of a misleading response will almost always be cause for instant dismissal, regardless of the amount of time elapsed since the declaration was made.

The handwritten covering letter

Many organizations still request that a handwritten covering letter accompanies the submission of a CV. It does appear that this is a declining request, in many instances simply due to the volumes of CVs received and the need to run the recruitment process as smoothly as possible.

Those organizations that do still request a covering letter do so for a number of reasons:

1 A handwritten document can provide information that doesn't appear on the CV. The letter usually details why the applicant is interested in the position and why, in their view, they are suitable for the position. This information tends

not to appear in the more traditional CV, which details a person's employment and educational history. However, the achievement-based CV will tend to provide such information within the Personal statement or Achievements section of the CV, largely making the covering letter redundant.

2 The letter goes some way in indicating to the employer that the applicant has made an effort to tailor their application to the position in question as it should make specific reference to the position being advertised by the organization. Of course, if you issue a standard covering letter to go with a generic CV to tens of employers, you will miss the whole point of the covering letter.

Whether it forms part of recruiting mythology or whether some organizations actually did this, it is said that handwriting experts would examine the script of the covering letter to determine further information about the applicant. If it were a commonly used tool, I suspect it is very much in decline today, due to the availability of profiling tests and applicant information available from a range of other sources online.

Summary

While the CV remains the key means of narrowing down candidates for a position, employers have an increasing range of other tools open to them in building up a profile of the applicant.

When applying for a role, it is no longer sufficient to focus on the content of your CV in isolation. You must consider the degree of consistency the information in your CV provides when compared to other sources of information available to the employing organization.

If in applying for your preferred roles you find that you are not reaching the interview stage, it may be that your skills and experience are not yet sufficient for that role. However, it may also be the case that the organization feels that your approach to working, or elements of your working style, is not compatible with the role for which you are applying. If you believe this is the case, it may be worth undertaking a personality or behaviour profiling test to gain a more comprehensive understanding of what types of role might be more aligned to your preferences.

Fact-check (answers at the back)

1. Potential employers:
   a) Use your CV as the only source of information about you ❏
   b) Ignore your CV and take more notice of what is said about you from references ❏
   c) Get most of their information about you from your online profile ❏
   d) Increasingly not only use your CV but also other sources of information, including online, to build up a picture of you ❏

2. Consistency across the various information sources available to the employer:
   a) Is something you should aim to achieve ❏
   b) Suggests you are boring and therefore unlikely to be selected ❏
   c) Is not an issue as potential employers should not be using anything other than your CV ❏
   d) All of the above ❏

3. The employer application form:
   a) Is now only available in an online format ❏
   b) Is used to prevent applicants from providing false information ❏
   c) Is now illegal due to anti-discrimination legislation ❏
   d) Is still used by many organizations in addition to your CV as it enables them to give more structure to the information they request from you ❏

4. In order to complete an application form effectively:
   a) Read the document several times before you complete it to understand what information is requested and in which section this should be placed ❏
   b) Read the job description carefully to help you make your answers relevant ❏
   c) Write out or type your answers first in draft on a separate sheet of paper and ask a friend or family member to review your draft answers ❏
   d) All of the above ❏

5. A handwritten covering letter:
   a) Is requested in cases where organizations wish to study the applicant's handwriting for clues to their personality ❏
   b) Can be a useful supporting document to indicate why an applicant believes they are suitable for a position and can add an extra dimension to the information provided ❏
   c) Is seen as old fashioned – all covering letters must now be produced by word processor to demonstrate computer literacy ❏
   d) Was last used successfully in 1998 ❏

6. When you are asked to undergo a profiling or personality test as part of an application:
a) You should answer the questions in the way you think the 'perfect applicant' should answer them ❏
b) You should refuse as this practice is seen as unethical ❏
c) Just be yourself and answer the questions truthfully and naturally ❏
d) You should answer in a way that is the opposite to what you really think as this makes the test results void ❏

7. It is useful for an organization to understand an applicant's preferred communication style:
a) As it provides some indication of how the person would interact with their manager and members of the team around them if successful ❏
b) So they know how to manipulate them at the interview stage ❏
c) As applicants who talk too much can be removed from the application process ❏
d) So their manager can get them to do things without them realizing it ❏

8. A 'fit and proper' questionnaire is generally used to find out:
a) Whether an applicant has a criminal record ❏
b) A person's financial position and creditworthiness ❏
c) Whether an applicant has been banned from holding a position of authority, such as Director of a company ❏
d) All of the above ❏

9. In completing a 'fit and proper' questionnaire:
a) You should answer the questions truthfully and honestly ❏
b) You should consult your legal adviser ❏
c) You should answer in a way that is not technically lying but does not necessarily tell a prospective employer the complete truth ❏
d) Your CV has indicated that you may have something to hide and the employer has issued this additional document ❏

10. If you find that you are generally unsuccessful in getting through to the interview stage:
a) Consider seeking advice from a person with experience in such matters, perhaps a manager you know who regularly reviews CVs ❏
b) Examine your online profile to see if there is anything that might possibly be putting potential employers off ❏
c) Try to get some feedback from organization or recruitment agencies you have approached on what you could improve ❏
d) All of the above ❏

SUNDAY

MONDAY

TUESDAY

WEDNESDAY

THURSDAY

FRIDAY

SATURDAY

FRIDAY

'Fuel injecting' your CV

Today we will look at steps you can take to improve the information contained within your CV and to increase the chances of you becoming successful in reaching the all-important interview stage of the recruitment process.

This chapter will cover the following aspects of 'fuel-injecting' your CV:

- Following a project-based approach to CV composition
- Specializing rather than generalizing
- Using a recruitment agency to your benefit
- Submitting CVs electronically

Following a project-based approach to CV composition

For individuals who operate within a mainly project-based environment, it is relatively straightforward to identify specific achievements, largely due to the fact that projects by definition possess structure, scope, budgets and timelines, against which that person's performance can be measured and determined. However, I have had discussions with a number of people who operate within non-project-based roles that are often referred to by the phrase 'business as usual'. This is the state of affairs within an organization or department where work is simply a continuation of tasks and undertaking of regular open-ended activities in line with the requirements of their role. The point being made by such individuals is that they find it difficult to express their achievements in quantifiable terms, since achievements are relatively difficult to identify when their work feels like one continuous process.

This is a valid point to raise. While more roles do contain a project-based component than before, this is not the case for everyone. For such individuals, I suggest that they examine their roles and activities more closely with a view to defining discrete components of their job that do contain project-like elements. A further step they can take is to volunteer for project-based work outside their day-to-day role.

Many organizations face rapid changes in their environment, regardless of the sector in which they operate, and are looking within their own organization for employees who can be seconded to projects. Taking part in such projects not only provides useful material for a future CV but genuinely stretches and expands the individual's skill set. A person who can demonstrate going outside their normal day-to-day role to gain further experience, project based or otherwise, will also be strengthening their CV for when it is required.

This area raises a further wider-reaching point. It is better to see your CV as a continuously developing document (remember the Latin definition as 'life path'), even when you do not need to use it.

TIP *Consider how you can strengthen your CV at regular intervals and do so by thinking about the types of activity in which you can become involved. Ask yourself how you can demonstrate proactivity and other desirable attributes long before you need to put your achievements to work in a submitted CV.*

Specializing rather than generalizing

It may be tempting to portray yourself as a generalist, being able to turn your hand to a wide range of roles. However, since the development of social media and other powerful means of communicating your skills to the relevant organizations, it is now much easier to let those who need your skills know that you exist, even if you are not immediately available. This is true to the extent now that a specialist in any part of the world can have their CV noticed by organizations on a truly global basis. Having a rare or deeply specialized occupation no longer means that the chances of moving roles are minimal.

As an example of this increased visibility and marketability of those in specialist roles, I have a very good friend who for many years worked in the UK as a hydrogen fuel cell scientist at the forefront of research into this extremely important area. Continuing quietly with his work, he was being increasingly contacted by organizations around the world keen to use his expertise. Dave has now moved with his family to Vancouver and, as well as having a fulfilling new job, he has a fantastic and well-balanced lifestyle.

Using a recruitment agency to your benefit

You may become involved with a recruitment agency in a range of circumstances, such as:

- when a specific role is publicized in a newspaper, magazine or journal and you are invited to submit your CV to a recruitment agency acting on behalf of a named or unnamed organization
- where, after initial correspondence directly with an organization, you are directed to send your CV to their preferred recruitment agency which handles a number of the initial stages of the process on their behalf
- where a recruitment organization invites the submission of CVs but does not mention a specific employer or role.

In the first two situations, you are applying for a particular position and the employer is outsourcing all or part of the recruitment process to a third-party recruitment specialist. In responding to such opportunities, you should follow the same approach that I advocate in making direct application to a potential employer.

There is often discussion around the possibility that recruitment agencies have their 'preferred candidates' or 'favourites' and that it is therefore difficult for an 'outsider' to get their CV in front of an employer. My view on this potential criticism of recruitment agencies, and I have no reason to support or criticize them, is that if agencies do have preferred candidates for some roles, such individuals have probably worked hard to get into such a position legitimately by structuring their CV effectively.

Many recruitment agencies specialize in particular sectors in which they have built up a reputation with its main employers. Furthermore, many organizations have a preference for one or two recruitment agencies with whom they have built up a relationship, sometimes over many years.

 TIP *To increase your chances of passing successfully through the recruitment agency 'filter', it is best to approach the recruitment organizations that tend to be regularly involved with the roles and organizations in which you are interested.*

Submitting CVs electronically

A significant number of organizations request the submission of CVs electronically. This enables them to:

● disseminate CVs to different personnel throughout the organization, often in different locations
● use search software to pick out relevant words or phrases of interest to them
● retain CVs for future positions, often loading them on to a database to enable future key word search.

Word search software

Use of word search software is an interesting development and one that you can use to your advantage. Potential employers and recruitment agencies who use this tool as part of their process claim that it helps them identify applicants who are more likely to be familiar with and experienced in the role in question. Their view is based on the premise that individuals with experience in that particular role are more likely to use specialist words or phrases in common usage by people who perform in that role. For example, a project manager may make reference to a particular type of software or methodology, or perhaps its abbreviated name, one that is only known to those who use it. Another example would be of an engineer or other technical specialist who may refer to a section of relevant legislation that would be known only to those who work within that environment.

TIP *To turn the word search method to your competitive advantage, include in your CV references to such specific components of the role that demonstrate your knowledge in this area. Of course, you must genuinely have experience in such matters, since you would soon be found lacking if questioned further at the interview stage.*

This point reinforces my belief that you should focus your efforts only on positions that require your skills and experience. As we have previously discussed, you can blend and emphasize your skills and experience depending on the requirements of the role (remember the Rubik's Cube analogy) but you should focus where your skills are strongest. If you are applying for a role that is different, on the face of it, from those you have undertaken in the past, you must work hard to show the transferability and applicability of the skills and experience you possess.

Even if word recognition software is not being used, the appropriate inclusion of specialist words or phrases within your CV will normally be noticed, thereby differentiating your CV, by those assessing your CV manually but who have a clear understanding of the requirements of the role.

File formats

When asked to submit your CV electronically, you will need to give some thought to the most appropriate format to use. If submitting by uploading to a potential employer or recruiter's site, you will normally be provided with instructions. The most common options are as a Word document or as a PDF document.

Word documents are generally acceptable to use but on occasion these can become distorted or lose formatting when opened by a recipient who does not have the same word-processing software, or even a different version of the same software. It is unfortunate if this happens, because a formatting problem can change the look of your CV. It is for this reason that many people prefer to send a PDF as it in effect 'takes a picture' of your document and shows it the way you intended it to be seen. The potential drawbacks of this route are that it can make the file size larger than the word document equivalent; it is more likely to get stuck in an organization's firewall or anti-virus software; or the recipient may not have the necessary PDF reader – although this is increasingly rare.

If you are following the advice in this book to keep the length of your CV to two pages and not to include a photograph, then you should not need to compress the file before sending it. However, if due to its size and the limits of the recipient's email inbox, you do need to compress the file, an application such as Winzip will suffice in such cases. As an alternative, you can always upload your file using such software as 'YouSendIt', which notifies the intended recipient where and how to download the file.

As mentioned in Tuesday's chapter in relation to recruitment agencies, it is advisable to speak to the prospective employer well before any deadline about the best option for submitting your CV electronically. I would also advise that you do not leave it until the last moment to do so as others may be doing the same, leading to online congestion.

The covering letter

A related question is whether you should submit an electronic letter with such submissions. Again, this depends on any guidance given by the prospective employer. If you feel that the personal statement within your CV does not sufficiently represent your cause, you may wish to submit a covering letter of no longer than three-quarters of a page and as a separate document to the CV, so that the recipient can deal with it separately to the CV if they wish. Should you have the scanning equipment to do so, you may wish to compose, print off and scan your letter as a PDF, and then sign it to give it that personal touch. As an alternative, your covering words can simply take the form of an email, which is wholly acceptable today and not seen as too informal.

Make sure that you acquire a sensible and professional email address when applying for jobs, preferably one containing your name, rather than the once amusing one you used as a teenager.

Summary

In a competitive jobs market, it is simply not sufficient to submit your CV to numerous organizations and 'hope for the best'. Organizations are becoming increasingly sophisticated in seeking out the most appropriately skilled and experienced people.

For their part, applicants must invest time and effort in analysing their own strengths and in communicating them effectively to organizations offering roles relevant to their skills and experience.

There are a number of steps you can take to increase the chances of matching your skills and experience profile to the roles you desire. You need to build and push your key messages through a number of routes and media, of which the CV is only one channel.

You also have to think ahead by seeing how your current roles and activities can be documented within a CV to show your suitability for new roles. You may need to decide what activities and roles to undertake if you are to be seen as shaping your career path. Passivity is unlikely to gain you access to the positions you desire.

SUNDAY

MONDAY

TUESDAY

WEDNESDAY

THURSDAY

FRIDAY

SATURDAY

Fact-check (answers at the back)

1. Having a specialism:
a) Is a disadvantage as it significantly limits the range of positions for which you can apply ❑
b) Is no barrier to job mobility, thanks to increased visibility through social media and business networking sites ❑
c) Is seen as old fashioned, with most employers preferring generalists ❑
d) Is a barrier to becoming a manager ❑

2. An advantage of being able to list project-type role experience is that:
a) Employers tend to employ people who have project management experience ❑
b) Such roles tend to have a stated objective, outcome, budget and other factors that can give a potential employer an indication of your performance ❑
c) You will be perceived as someone who 'gets ahead' in life ❑
d) You will get an automatic increase in your starting salary ❑

3. In this context, the abbreviation BAU stands for:
a) Before Applicant Understanding ❑
b) Behaviour Attitude ❑
c) Business As Usual ❑
d) Business Audit Unit ❑

4. Using a recruitment agency:
a) Is seen as a sign of desperation by potential employers and as such should be avoided ❑
b) Will guarantee you an interview, as they know the system ❑
c) Will result in you getting a smaller starting salary than applying directly, in order to pay the agency's commission ❑
d) Can be helpful, as you may get advice on how to structure your CV and on the types of role best suited to your skills and experience ❑

5. Many recruitment agencies:
a) Specialize in particular sectors ❑
b) Have built up a relationship and reputation with their key clients ❑
c) Have advisers who can help with your CV ❑
d) All of the above ❑

6. A recruitment organization inviting CVs but making no mention of a specific employer or role:
a) Is operating illegally ❑
b) Is recruiting for the security services and is not permitted to give details of the role ❑
c) Is likely to be gathering a pool of potential candidates for future use but has not been asked to recruit for a specific role ❑
d) Will only match you with a potential employer if you pay a fee ❑

7. The use of electronic CVs can have advantages for an employer, in that:

a) It enables them to circulate CVs to different personnel throughout the organization, often in different locations ❏

b) It allows them to use search software to pick out key words likely to be contained in relevant CVs ❏

c) It helps them to keep a record of unsuccessful applicants for a particular role, but who may be more suited to a future position ❏

d) All of the above ❏

8. Including key words or phrases in your CV that are specific to your role:

a) Is likely to be seen as unnecessary use of jargon and will lead to your CV being rejected ❏

b) Indicates you do not really know what you are talking about and have just copied them from the job description ❏

c) When done carefully can lead to your CV being 'flagged' by key word search software, as an indicator that you have experience in a particular role or specialism ❏

d) Is a form of cheating and is not to be recommended ❏

9. The following behaviours are likely to be viewed positively by a potential employer:

a) Proactive management of your career to date ❏

b) Criticizing previous employers ❏

c) Making it clear that the position you are applying for is only a temporary arrangement until something more suitable comes along ❏

d) Making suggestions when you first meet them on how to improve their recruitment process ❏

10. The following behaviours are likely to be viewed negatively by a potential employer:

a) Striving to make all sources of information about you consistent and accurate ❏

b) Looking to present yourself as 'You at your best' ❏

c) Being truthful, honest and frank about both your skills and your areas of development ❏

d) Doing whatever it takes to get the job ❏

SUNDAY

MONDAY

TUESDAY

WEDNESDAY

THURSDAY

FRIDAY

SATURDAY

SATURDAY

Managing your online profile

As well as the paper version of your CV, it is likely that you will also have left evidence of your profile online, either intentionally or without realizing it.

Until this century, other than following up references supplied by you or having an informal conversation with a contact at your current organization, the only source of information initially open to a recruiting organization was contained within your CV.

Now, with a range of social media available to them, an increasing number of organizations review these sources in addition to the CV itself. Today we look at the impact of social media sites on the information presented in a CV and how employers are using such information to cross-check information contained in CVs. We'll focus on:

- the ethical debate
- LinkedIn
- Facebook
- 'blogging' sites
- Twitter
- search engines
- review sites and news sites.

The ethical debate

There is some debate as to the ethics of using social media sites as a means of supplementing the information available from your CV. Many would argue that social media sites belong to the family and leisure side of life and as such should not be used for work-related reasons. They would also say that the veracity of such sources cannot be assumed, particularly if comments were not posted by the job applicant themselves.

Those on the other side of the argument would suggest that the information on social media sites provides a useful supplementary perspective on you as a person. Additionally, while the CV provides a snapshot of your situation, social media sites indicate various aspects of your character over time and are arguably a better insight into your qualities than the (one would assume) carefully worded content of your CV.

As an applicant, you should always assume that a prospective employer, or recruitment agency acting on their behalf, will at some stage look at your online presence.

There are therefore grey areas in what information employers think is acceptable to take from social networking sites, but most organizations would be comfortable taking into account information from a business networking site such as LinkedIn – in effect treating your entry as an additional online CV. It is important, therefore, that you do actively manage your profile on such sites to ensure that the information you present is consistent with what you provide in your submitted CV.

What this means to any and all of us who are likely in future to apply for an employed position, as well as self-employed individuals seeking work from other organizations, is that ongoing management and care of your online persona is vitally important.

Let's now take a look at what types of online information in social media and other sites may have a bearing on how potential employers see you.

LinkedIn

This increasingly popular business-related social networking site is well used by people in work across the world, both as a means of creating an online profile and for networking with people in a similar type of work or sector.

In addition to profiles of individuals, there are an increasing number of organizational profiles, often linking to people who have previously been employed by them.

There is a high degree of usage of this site among recruitment agencies and organizations looking to employ personnel, a proportion of whom use the premium package enabling them to search across and communicate with all individuals profiled on the site, not just those they know ('are LinkedIn to').

How to manage your LinkedIn profile

- Keep your profile up to date and current.
- Put the job role or skill set you most want to be known for in the primary description. It is this field that shows up when a searching organization uses a key word search to identify a potential pool of people for a vacant role.
- If you elect to attach a photograph of yourself to your LinkedIn profile (many people do), use one that shows you in a professional light – in other words, not one of you enjoying yourself at a recent party.
- Keep all comments and updates you make to this site professional.

Facebook

As the most used social network in the world, this site needs little introduction. Anyone you know under the age of 30 has a page on this site, as do increasing numbers over this age. With its undoubted benefits to people in keeping connected with one another in a personal capacity, it does carry some risk if personal information and comments 'leak' into the world of work. There have been a number of cases in the media of individuals being disciplined or even dismissed by their employer due to negative comments or details of activities incompatible with their employment becoming known to their employer.

How to manage your Facebook profile

- Ensure that your privacy settings are set to the level of exposure you require. You may be surprised at the high number of people who have open settings, allowing people they don't know, as well as their employer, to view their Facebook pages. Bear in mind that with your privacy setting at 'Everyone', this means not just everyone on Facebook but everyone with access to the Internet.
- Review images tagged to your name on a regular basis to find out whether there are any photographs of a negative nature associated with you in this way. You may have adequate privacy controls on your Facebook page but your friends may not. Even if you think there are no images on the site showing you in a negative light, it is useful to know whether there are negative images linked to a person with the same name as you. These may be seen by a possible employer who mistakenly believes the image to be of you.

'Blogging' sites

Such sites, shortened from 'web log', generally take the form of online journals, diaries or day-to-day observations of anyone who cares to post them online. These can be immensely interesting and, indeed, entertaining. However, many are extremely opinionated and statements made can at times veer into the slanderous and occasionally malicious. This is of course the prerogative of the 'blogger'. However, opinions you shared and views you offered some time in the past may be incompatible with the employment roles that you may now be seeking.

 TIP *While in no way wishing to restrict anyone's right to free speech, it is wise to carefully consider what you write and how it may be perceived by a potential employer in the future.*

Twitter

Twitter is what is known as a 'micro-blogging' site through which you can instantly send your thoughts to the world in short messages of up to 140 characters. As many in the public eye have found to their cost, it is very tempting to message on Twitter (known as 'tweeting') in response to a hot topic or to someone else's message and come to regret your words later.

While it is possible to remove your previous messages, it is also possible that they may have been captured by someone else or forwarded to others ('retweeted') and therefore continue to exist on the Internet in association with your name.

Search engines

If you have never done so, you may be surprised by what comes up if you search for your name using an Internet search engine. Much of what appears will relate to people with the same name as you (which can lead to misinformation in itself). You may also find references to comments you have made, or attributed to you, that you would rather a potential employer did not see.

There is little you can do about search engine entries without spending a fair amount of time or money investing in help to push such entries further down the search pages. The best course of action is a pre-emptive one in managing your online presence to reduce the likelihood of a negative comment relating to you appearing on the first few pages of an online search of your name. It is worth noting that such a search can pick up images as well as written comments, reinforcing the need to maintain the correct level of privacy settings on your social networking sites.

Review sites and news sites

Even people who are careful in managing their online presence may miss this one. If you have ever left a review of a hotel, a car hire firm or anything else on either their site or a third-party review site, for example TripAdvisor, in your own name, the chances are it will appear in the results of an Internet search of your name. If the review was particularly negative or contained strong language, such an entry may create an adverse impression if seen by a potential employer.

The popularity of a site (i.e. the amount of Internet traffic it receives) will determine to an extent how visible your comment becomes, with high traffic-flow sites being particularly prominent. The message again is to think carefully before making such comments, taking into account the impact they may have on your online reputation and on anyone in the future who may use the Internet to build a further impression of your character or your tendency to comment on, for example, previous employers.

Similarly to review sites, any comments you make in your own name in relation to an online news story could come to the attention of a potential employer. Commenting strongly on press stories, particularly ones that divide opinion, while perfectly within your rights in most territories, can be perceived negatively by prospective employers.

 TIP *Consider the potential impact on your online reputation of any comments you make on review sites and news sites.*

Summary

Gone are the days when you could manage how a potential employer perceives you by controlling what went into your CV and how you presented yourself at interview.

Your cumulative online presence creates an increasing amount of material to help an organization piece together additional information on your character and activities. Of course, there are dangers in an organization using such information, both in terms of accuracy and in stepping over the line between a person's private life and their work. However, as we have mentioned, many believe that if you 'put it out there' then they are entitled to take it into account when assessing your suitability for a position with them.

Overall then, the key message is that the information you provide, either intentionally or unintentionally, makes an impression on those who are in a position to offer you a new role. Keep this in mind when you interact online and every time you consider posting a comment, considering how this might be perceived in the future.

Fact-check (answers at the back)

1. The contents of your online profile:
    a) Are your own business and no one, least of all a potential employer, has any business prying through it ❑
    b) Should be recognized as a potential source of additional information about you and, as such, managed carefully ❑
    c) Cannot be controlled, so why bother? ❑
    d) Get erased every six months ❑

2. LinkedIn is:
    a) A business networking site that also allows you to include your resumé ❑
    b) A dating site ❑
    c) Only available to people working in commerce ❑
    d) Run by a cartel of recruitment agencies ❑

3. A particularly useful aspect of LinkedIn is that:
    a) Skills and experience mentioned in your headline profile appear in key word searches ❑
    b) It is increasingly monitored by potential employers and recruitment agencies alike ❑
    c) It is free to use at its basic level ❑
    d) All of the above ❑

4. Twitter is:
    a) A social networking site, therefore potential employers are legally obliged to ignore anything you say on it ❑
    b) A social networking (micro-blogging) site that enables anyone to make brief comments in real time (including when tired, emotional or drunk) ❑
    c) What birds do, so why is it relevant to this subject? ❑
    d) Set up in a way that lets only people you allow to see what you say ❑

5. Facebook:
    a) For a fee, will allow organizations to review your entire profile regardless of your privacy settings ❑
    b) Has introduced a 'timeline' component to profiles which, if not managed, could reveal past activities that you'd rather a potential employer didn't discover ❑
    c) Is now the preferred means of creating and submitting CVs in Scotland ❑
    d) Will automatically generate your CV for you, using material you have posted ❑

6. Online images of you:
a) Cannot be identified if they don't have your name on them ❑
b) Will not influence someone considering employing you ❑
c) Can still identify you if a search of your name pulls up an image that someone has tagged with your name ❑
d) Only underline how professional you are at all times ❑

7. When you write online reviews of products or services you have used:
a) These may still be seen years after you made them ❑
b) These may appear high up in a search engine list, due to volume of traffic to the original site ❑
c) You should work on the basis that a future employer may read them ❑
d) All of the above ❑

8. Organizations that ask you to submit your CV online via their website:
a) Will give preference to such applications over those sent by post ❑
b) Will give preference to documents submitted in hard copy ❑
c) Are increasing in number, so it is advisable to familiarize yourself with such a process ❑
d) Insist your document is protected using 128-bit encryption ❑

9. Anything you read online about a potential employer:
a) Is likely to be true ❑
b) Is only put there by disgruntled former employees ❑
c) Can be useful in helping you prepare for the interview process but treat with caution ❑
d) Will also be known to them ❑

10. At www.cvl.co.uk/cvexamples, you will find examples of
a) Good CVs ❑
b) Bad CVs ❑
c) Job descriptions ❑
d) Covering letters ❑

7 × 7

1 Seven trends for tomorrow

- A successful CV stays current and reflects how the world is changing.
- Use of online CVs such as LinkedIn is increasing.
- Employers are looking for more multilingual employees.
- Jobs for life continue to decline, so think of yourself as 'Me Co.' or 'Me Inc.' with skills and experience for hire – in both the long and short term.
- New technology is driving change, with the increasing use of automated CV grammar and spell checkers at first sift. Will hologram CVs be the next thing?
- We'll have a longer working life as a result of our increased life expectancy. Consider developing skills and experience for next phase of your working life, doing something completely different.
- Prospective employers are looking for more succinct CVs, so make yours short and snappy (and two pages at most).

2 Seven great organizations worth working for

- PricewaterhouseCoopers, www.pwc.co.uk
- KPMG, www.kpmg.com
- Apple Inc., www.apple.com/uk
- UNHCR, www.unhcr.org.uk
- Google, www.google.co.uk
- Médecins sans Frontières, www.msf.org.uk
- [Insert your name here] Incorporated/Limited

3 Seven things to do today

- Manage your career and your CV proactively – it keeps you motivated. Ask someone who employs or recruits for a local employer to review your CV and give you honest feedback (you never know, it may give you an opening).
- Check the spelling and grammar in your CV. This is vital. Then get someone else to do it again.
- Check that your Facebook settings are not public – those 'party photos' may put off prospective employers.
- Consider having your LinkedIn photograph professionally taken – a portrait in business dress appropriate for your sector works best generally.
- Check what's out there about you on Google and other search engines, including images. Manage your online presence.
- In your current role, take on new challenges and consider additional qualifications. Recent additions to your CV generally impress, showing that you continue to develop yourself.
- Stay positive. There's a role out there for you – your future employer just doesn't know about you yet.

4 Seven inspirational people who probably didn't need a CV

- Einstein – He was not seen as being clever by his teachers; all relative, I suppose.
- Bill Gates – He saw an opportunity and made the most of it.
- Edith Cavell – Look her up. Hers is an amazing story of courage and selflessness.
- Steve Jobs – He had a vision where others didn't, and saw it through.
- Ghandi – This was a true leader who knew what his people needed.

- Nelson Mandela – He lived with a clear purpose and great dignity.
- The best teacher or mentor you ever had – If it's not too late, let them know.

5 Seven words and phrases to avoid in your CV (and what employers think of them)

- 'Motivated self-starter' – I will be the judge of that when I see what your timekeeping is like.
- 'Passionate' – This is one of the most inappropriately used adjectives, particularly when preceding 'about bookkeeping' or similar. Keep it real.
- 'Huge leadership potential' – You don't seem to have found anyone to lead yet.
- 'Capability to work unsupervised' – You wish.
- 'Creative talent' – You mean you don't like doing the boring day-to-day stuff.
- 'Can speak conversational Spanish/French' – You can order a coffee or a beer in a bar.
- 'Popular with managers and colleagues alike' – Hmmm.

6 Seven core skills every potential employer would like to see in a CV

- Effective communicator: you get across your point as accurately and efficiently as possible, recognizing that other people have different communication styles and preferences (some get to the point quickly, others are born storytellers). Communication style isn't an indicator of intelligence.

- Good decision maker: you can make the right decision, even where there is ambiguity in a situation and the guidance doesn't wholly cover it.
- Team player: you have an ability to work effectively with the people around you, including customers, colleagues, suppliers and supervisors.
- Ethical: you do the right thing ethically and morally.
- Self-aware: you know your limitations and can identify areas for development and do something about them.
- Empathic: you take into account the needs, feelings and aspirations of others in the decisions you make and actions you take.
- Modest: You are able to take honestly offered feedback in the spirit it was intended and use it to be better at what you do.

7 Seven aspirational entries in the CV of your life

- Learned all I could from my parents, friends, colleagues and teachers
- Matched my talents, energy and experience to roles, not being afraid to move or change when it didn't work out
- Passed on my accumulated knowledge and experience to those who were ready to receive it, without expectation of reward and with no agenda
- Travelled as much as I could, seeking out different cultures and experiences (for example, going to the opera at least once)
- Didn't stress about issues or situations over which I had no control
- Stayed true to myself while remaining sensitive to the feelings of others
- Regretted nothing (helped by making the most of my time on this wonderful planet and making good life decisions along the way)

Answers

Sunday: 1b; 2d; 3b; 4b; 5d; 6c; 7a; 8b; 9b; 10a

Monday: 1a; 2c; 3c; 4b; 5c; 6b; 7a; 8b; 9a; 10a

Tuesday: 1d; 2c; 3b; 4b; 5d; 6b; 7b; 8a; 9b; 10a

Wednesday: 1d; 2a; 3b; 4c; 5b; 6a; 7a; 8b; 9b; 10d

Thursday: 1d; 2a; 3d; 4d; 5b; 6c; 7a; 8d; 9a; 10d

Friday: 1b; 2b; 3c; 4d; 5d; 6c; 7d; 8c; 9a; 10d

Saturday: 1b; 2a; 3d; 4b; 5b; 6c; 7d; 8c; 9c; 10 See the website for examples of all of these

ALSO AVAILABLE IN THE 'IN A WEEK' SERIES

APPRAISALS • BRAND MANAGEMENT • BUSINESS PLANS • CONTENT MARKETING • COVER LETTERS • DIGITAL MARKETING • DIRECT MARKETING • EMOTIONAL INTELLIGENCE • FINDING & HIRING TALENT • JOB HUNTING • LEADING TEAMS • MARKET RESEARCH • MARKETING • MBA • MOBILE MARKETING • NETWORKING • OUTSTANDING CONFIDENCE • PEOPLE MANAGEMENT • PLANNING YOUR CAREER • PROJECT MANAGEMENT • SMALL BUSINESS MARKETING • STARTING A NEW JOB • TACKLING TOUGH INTERVIEW QUESTIONS • TIME MANAGEMENT

For information about other titles in the 'In A Week' series, please visit www.teachyourself.co.uk

MORE TITLES AVAILABLE IN THE 'IN A WEEK' SERIES

ADVANCED NEGOTIATION SKILLS • ASSERTIVENESS • BUSINESS ECONOMICS • COACHING • COPYWRITING • DECISION MAKING • DIFFICULT CONVERSATIONS • ECOMMERCE • FINANCE FOR NON-FINANCIAL MANAGERS • JOB INTERVIEWS • MANAGING STRESS AT WORK • MANAGING YOUR BOSS • MANAGING YOURSELF • MINDFULNESS AT WORK • NEGOTIATION SKILLS • NLP • PEOPLE SKILLS • PSYCHOMETRIC TESTING • SEO AND SEARCH MARKETING • SOCIAL MEDIA MARKETING • START YOUR OWN BUSINESS • STRATEGY • SUCCESSFUL SELLING • UNDERSTANDING AND INTERPRETING ACCOUNTS

For information about other titles in the 'In A Week' series, please visit
www.teachyourself.co.uk

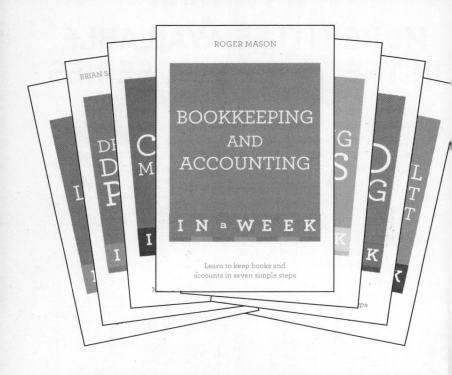

YOUR FASTEST ROUTE TO SUCCESS

LEARN IN A WEEK WHAT THE EXPERTS LEARN IN A LIFETIME

For information about other titles
in the 'In A Week' series, please visit
www.teachyourself.co.uk